Spectral Realms

No. 6 ‡ Winter 2017

Edited by S. T. Joshi

The spectral realms that thou canst see
With eyes veil'd from the world and me.

H. P. LOVECRAFT, "To a Dreamer"

SPECTRAL REALMS is published twice a year by Hippocampus Press,
P.O. Box 641, New York, NY 10156 (www.hippocampuspress.com).
Copyright © 2017 by Hippocampus Press.
All works are copyright © 2017 by their respective authors.
Cover artwork by Dugald Stewart Walker (1883–1937) for
Hans Christian Andersen's "What the Moon Saw" (1840; rpt. 1914).
Cover design by Barbara Briggs Silbert.
Hippocampus Press logo by Anastasia Damianakos.

ISBN 978-1-61498-191-6   ISSN 2333-4215

Contents

Poems

Spider Eggs

John Shirley

Some infant spiders quickly hatch,
emerge at a week, or less;
some eight-legged babes take wintry months
to finally undress.
But certain secret spider eggs
are by scientists unseen;
For they're composed of astral stuff,
more difficult to glean.
More perilous than spiders
Ma Nature ever spun:
These eggs are laid by meanness
—and it cannot be undone.
Sometimes it's a casual crime,
a cruel and scarring word;
maybe a sly and slashing blade,
a swish that's never heard.
It may be abandonment,
as many children know:
for a child is a harvester
who reaps what others sow.
These eggs are laid by evil deeds
in damp and grimy shadows
(some hide deep like funnel spiders;
others glitter like black widows).
"It's done," folk claim, "it's past and gone—

only water 'neath the bridge!"
—Even as these spiders incubate
'neath bed and under fridge.
For they are more than symbol—
no mere metaphor;
they're actual beings ripening
till time for creeping forth.
Invisible they creep and hunch,
unseeable but felt;
you look, then think it wasn't real—
but later find the welt.
They feed and grow, outspreading like
an ancient dying tree;
looming webs of sticky black
make light cursed hard to see.
These spider eggs may even be
hidden in your bones:
I mean the eggs that hatch within
to rejoice in your groans.
Consider then the consequence
of a selfish, mindless act—
Lest your choice lay spider's eggs . . .
that will not fail to crack.

Edgar A. Poe (1809–1849)

W. H. Pugmire

An arsenical moon hangs in suicidal sky,
Which I would drink like laudanum,
And to which I would add crushed pearls of starlight.
Night-wind soughs in moving trees
And sounds like a rustling of purple curtains,
Like the mating of raven wings.
I wander the place of tombs where Helen walked—
I stroll alone. Come, take my spectral hand,
I pray you, and move with me
Through silence, memory, and torment.

Finite

Ian Futter

Everything dies.

Even the maggots
and even the flies
that feed on the corpses
and chew out their eyes.

Everything dies.

Even volcanoes
that rumble and rise
to spew out their life fire
into the skies.

Everything dies.

Even your love
and that look of surprise.
Even blind passion,
that's fear in disguise.

Everything dies.

Excepting the hatred
and all of those lies;
like dark stars collapsing
to dust in the skies.

Everything dies.

Oracle

Wade German

What were the things you meant to say
Before you left for other lands,
Those distant regions, dim and grey,
To dwell amid eternal sands
That know not night, nor break of day—
That twilight realm without a sun,
The kingdom of oblivion?

Hear you, that we would here receive
The mysteries that you can tell
Of worlds beyond, but few believe?
Hither to us and doubt dispel,
If only for a while to leave
Your house in Hell untenanted—
Come whisper wisdom of the dead.

Next

John J. Mundy

The animals are coming!
The animals are coming–

And what variety! What exotic diversity!
Choose your fate, your destiny–
Mock piety on stealthy padded feet
Cupidity in a purring caress.
The sagacity of serpents swallow all doubt
Goat-things rut to inflame your lust;
A strange and fabulous bestiary stirs
from the shadows of your heart,
The Children you nurtured and raised
Not griffin hydra hellhound lamia gorgon
A throng now obsolete, deserving of dust
You burned the old books of fable and myth
Tame for one of your tastes . . .

Make way! O, make way,
For dark and shining creatures triumphant!
Greet the new and novel!
The scales fur claws fangs feathers fins
The slithering instruments of vengeance
The abominations you alone nursed
O the animals are coming
And you foolishly invited them in
Opening your heart to their pitiless lust

Your free ranging children have all come home
And on fresh flesh they will feast
For how could you refuse them
Their loyalty was beyond reproach
They have feasted on your friends and loved ones
Gained strength from blood of enemies
Now be magnanimous
And let them dine.

The Fateful Flower

Frank Coffman

The hyacinth was far her favorite flower,
Especially those of purple hue and blue,
Symbolic of their love sworn ever true.
It grew thick 'round the confines of her bower.

One day she looked out from her castle tower
Just then to see her lover come in view—
But there—alas! beside him—someone new!
They kissed.
             Then her expression grew most dour.
Faithless he was! Her heart turned instant cold.

She mixed a potion, horrible and dire.
Wronged sorceress, she'd not be left alone!
Fungi most leprous, the skin of a toad,
Nightshade and hemlock, venoms cursed of old:
One sip would make his belly turn to fire.
But one taste and he'd ail in flesh and bone,
And horrid boils of pus and blood explode.
His noble features, beauteous of old,
Would change most terribly. Then he'd expire
In agony.
           And, when the deed was done,
And she the awful changes did behold,
She pierced the fickle heart with a small knife
Of that false man who'd promised her to wife.

Then—drew the blade across her snow-white throat
And joined him. And her spirit too was thrown
Into that realm of darkness far remote.

Whether they met again cannot be known.
But on her marker, with blue blossoms overstrown,
The engraver with his fine keen chisel smote
Hyacinthine flourishes into the cold, hard stone.

Vul Ravin

D. L. Myers

Vul Ravin,
Forest of endings,
Where all light comes to naught
And every path is swarmed by peril.
All things immense, virulent and fatal
Seek the flame of life on which to feast,
And every organism seeks to savor
The merest glimmer of its illumination.
Lurid blossoms in an opalescent dance of hues
Hide viperous spines whose bite brings
Frenzy, sweat-bright lunacy and death,
And the silence is ever fractured by cries
While gyring forms fill the air with slaughter.

A hungry forest of titanic black trees,
Teems with quills and talons, spikes and teeth;
Leagues of life insatiable, ever prowling.
Only death finds comfort here,
In quiet pools poisonously colored
And lined with ageless bones,
Upon whose mirrored surfaces
No human eye has stared,
No mortal mind has grasped,

Or realized more than fear.
Vul Ravin,
Forest of terror.
Vul Ravin,
Forest of death.

Transfiguration

Ronald Terry

We who have descended
know neither love nor hate.
We will not overcome you;
we will transform you into ourselves.

Our god is a bloody torso,
its head long sacrificed
to animate our fantasy of life.

We walk among you,
born aloft,
embedded into your scaffold.
We will send you without death
to our god, not yours.

To sight, we are vaporous
and insubstantial.
Our reality depends
on your ability to dream.

Seeds are buried
in the black soil
at the core of mind.

This is our birth
into your world
as your heads turn
inside out into our children.

Mistress of the Dark Fortress

K. A. Opperman and Leigh Blackmore

I. The Sorceress

By K. A. Opperman

It looms beyond the dreams of gods and men—
A thousand-towered fortress wrought of jet,
Whose onyx peaks and bastions are beset
By violet levins ever and again.

Gigantic gargoyles ward its dreadful walls,
Their yawning gullets tongued with sanguine flames;
A lovely voice calls out their secret names,
And they awake to watch the haunted halls.

For one has stumbled through the sable waste
To win the heart of her who dwells within—
A sorceress with lips as red as sin,
Whose gemmy fingers countless charms have traced.

As she observes her blood-filled scrying bowl,
Her bosom trembles with a stifled laugh
To see this hero—not her match by half—
Attempt to gain her heart, a hopeless goal.

A knight in armor, bent against the blast
Of winds that blow beyond the realm of time,

Assails her fortress and begins to climb
The serpent-holden steps that few have passed.

So she begins to weave an evil spell,
One that would chill his soul and pierce his heart—
But she is thwarted in her witch's art
By splashing toads inside the mantic well.

The scene obscured, she loses sight of him,
So she upturns the purple porphyry;
The vessel shatters, leaking sorcery—
Lamenting daemons, moaning seraphim.

Her raven hair disheveled, her simar
Of scarlet silk scarce clothing luscious breasts,
Upon the balcon, at her screamed behests,
There lights her gargoyle, 'neath a greenish star.

II. The Gargoyle and the Knight

By Leigh Blackmore

Its wings unfurled, its loathly maw agape,
It snarls and flaps, a daemon soul possessed;
Her upthrust hand caresses its rough crest,
Its name she whispers, soothes its hateful shape.

By secret words, its movements she commands;
No knight shall breach her gate or keep this night.
She sends the thing aloft in monstrous flight
To seek the knight who dares these shadowlands.

As far below, the errant knight fights on,
From sabatons to crowning burgonet
Protected by his scales of silvered fret,
With sword unsheathed against the devil's spawn.

Down swoops the creature, venting shrieking cry.
The bidding of its mistress made it moan
Since first it came to this unhallowed zone;
It drops upon him darkly from on high.

He wills to win the fiendish sorceress;
With blade upraised, he slashes at his foe;
He strikes the thing a savage killing blow,
Severs its scaled head—so far, success!

She views his triumph, yet with no alarm,
As on he clambers, to the umbral tower
Wherein she stands, resplendent in her power;
Urged on by lust, the knight discounts her charm—

Which transformed men to vicious, ghastly brutes;
All gargoyles here, enchanted by her spells
Were once like him—men risking lofty hells
To taste the sorceress and her sweet fruits.

And as he enters in her splendid den,
She casts the spell that always serves her ends;
He staggers once, and falls, as she intends
And tumbling to the stones, he loses ken.

So, bending down, she whispers in his ear
Bestows on him a secret, mystic name;
His birth-name fades; she lays her awful claim
To snare his soul; he sheds a silent tear.

III. Epilogue

On sheer obsidian keeps, gargoyles stand guard;
A grotesque thing, unmanned, broods there this night.
What ill fate cursed a foolish, gallant knight
Abandoned here, enslaved, forever scarred?

Un-Hallowed E'en

Richard L. Tierney

This is the night when graveyard gates
    Creak open of their own accord.
    Within, with glittering scythe and sword,
The black-cowled Reaper grimly waits.

From His skull-sockets red stars glare
    Upon His dead yet wakening slaves
    Who lurch new-risen from their graves
At His command. Now, forth they fare

Into each darkened street and lane
    To do the bidding of their King—
    To stalk, to slay, and then to bring
New lifeless slaves to His domain.

The Reaper's laughter, deep and grim,
    Rings from His yellowed skull with glee,
    For well He knows the Time shall be
When all mankind are brought to Him.

Diluvian Night Out

Jessica Amanda Salmonson

There's a road down there that rolls into the sea
We can drive below unto the lost city
In our bullet-nosed Studebaker sub
To a parking lot by Sinker's Pub.

And in that pub a Celtic drum
Is beaten by a sailor dead
He beats it with a bony thumb
And hums a dirge of loss and dread.

Upon the roof there sits a king
With lolling tongue and lidless eyes
Who burbles as he strives to sing
And longs for death but never dies.

There's a soda shop run by a squid
With a Panoram jukebox playing Oh You Kid
They've triple scoop cones with a crab on top
And urchin on a stick like a lollipop.

Those ocean lights are from a snack bar stand
And the outdoor screen, we can park on sand
The film they're showing is "Far to the Lee"
Starring Billy Ocean and Daniella Sea.

An after hour club called Atlantis Bound
With an orchestra of musicians drowned
On the Titanic in a bygone age
When the Turkey Trot was all the rage.

C'mon, let's turkey trot,
Gobble-diddle-ip, Gobble-gobble diddle-ip
Do a little shimmy and get me hot
Grab a little ebb tide, let her rip.

Chrysalides in the Cromlech

Jeff Burnett

I slog through thornen brakes and swampy hells
With gaiety, unscathed by mossy fang;
But lo! when pale Luna gravid swells
With glamoury, the spider's silk enchains
The wandering foot to midnight's blackest banes.
The siren sings with hemlock-honeyed breath
And beckons me with eyes of emerald death.

Of brooding mind I tread the meadows, bask
With adders drowsing 'neath the amber rays
Of morn; but lo! the incandescent mast
Of Sol's bright galley bursts into white flames:
My skull an iron furnace to my brain.
As midnight suckles imps of aconite,
The noontide harbors dooms of lily-white.

Betwixt the ivory pyres and ebon webs
I creep into a cromlech, ruminate;
But lo! phantasmagoria rears its head:
Lilac sprites with roots of mandrake mate,
The scorpion and the butterfly mutate
To join as lovers ever in the dusk,
Transcend the Sun, the Moon, their Earth-born husks.

When the Stars Are Right

Oliver B. Harris

It happened at a time when society had ground to a halt just as it accelerated virtually to the point of singularity, like a gerbil in a wheel, running ever faster and faster, expending its life's blood in going precisely nowhere. Televised news reports had become indistinguishable from the programmes that ostensibly parodied them; the people laughed aloud at the words of politicians and took the pronouncements of comedians as deadly serious analysis; holy men were caught with whores and catamites on a weekly basis while the words of athletes were revered as if they were prophets and sibyls.

Governments fought wars against the groups they'd armed the week before and jihadis destroyed the fast food joints where they'd taken their first dates four years previously. The sciences made the distinctions between man and beast and between matter and information more porous and diaphanous with each passing month; space probes whispered the echoes of secrets from the womb of Time and those who listened to them shuddered and doubted themselves, while their colleagues in adjacent departments reknitted the stuff of Life to recipes sponsored by pharmaceutical industrialists. The seasons were horribly mixed, and the birds, beasts, and fish swarmed this way and that in a fashion that perplexed the greatest authorities on living things; those who staffed the asylums began to fear that their patients displayed not insanity but super-sanity, a new form of intellect fit to understand this new phase of existence, terrifying to the old order that could not comprehend it.

The rumors of great change, greater by far than the changes society wrought on itself, began to be exchanged online, in furtive whispers from people who doubted even themselves for madmen, yet all knew that the things they'd felt while alone in the dead of night or while caught in great surging crowds of fellow commuters spoke truly as harbingers of unheard-of transitions. And then the real changes began, great stirrings within the water and land as of colossal creatures exercising muscles long unused but still imbued with primordial strength. The cities of men began to crumble and totter as the earth beneath them buckled, not from blind seismic happenstance but from a conscious realignment of soil, bedrock, tectonic plate. Rivers rose up from their beds and bent and twisted deliriously in their air; forests marched upon the settlements of men and slew them wantonly; the beasts of field and barn turned on those who tended them, and devoured them.

And in the midst of all this, the Great Old Ones awoke once more, slithering upon the land from their beds at the depths of the sea, surging up through great pits in the earth, emerging from the hearts of forests, deserts and mountains and seeping down from space. For now the stars were right again, and on They came in unstoppable waves. Those who still lived no longer doubted the words of the prophets, and were too stricken with madness even to scream or run or try to hide themselves, but laughed uproariously as one who has suddenly understood a joke that seemed for a lifetime to be no more than a mistake or discrepancy. Chaos crawled hither and thither and delighted in all It saw.

Soon They had utter mastery of the waters and the air, the earth, the cities and wild places alike. Now Earth was their plaything, and since the laws of man and the cosmos no longer applied, they made such sport of it as they desired.

The Dust That Was You

Mary Krawczak Wilson

Yours is the voice I cannot hear
The wind screeches—it strives to reach me
It muffles out the howling in the trees
And keeps you from being near.

Yours is the face I cannot see
The snow falls steadily and unceasingly
It snuffs out all colors greedily
And leaves you folded in its frozen scree.

Yours is the essence I cannot smell
The relentless rain rides roughshod
Over the fields, plains, and sod
And drowns you in its rancid hell.

Yours is the body I cannot touch
The earth shudders and quakes
It digs out everything in its wake
And covers you in the dust of its clutch.

Hunted

Claire Smith

You're on the hunt for a tiger
And the promise of a trophy.
You spot me, creep in my direction,
Your feet squelch on the dew-drop grass.
I've disappeared before you can catch
Me, my shadow melts into the swamp mist.

The promise of a tiger's pelt pushes
You onward, so you take no notice
Of the warning sign: DANGER!
Accompanied by a barbed-wire threat
You hear a song—
My voice weaves its way out of the fog.

Lyrics sung to allure you, in a tenor's tone
Reveal a man—my new transformation.
You feel your way to my siren's call.
I'm the oasis of the rainforest, I'm everything:
From its mulch carpeted floor,
To lush ferns, to the treetop canopy.

You stumble into my quicksand trap
Mesmerised and sinking, you call for help.
But you're stuck. I'm a chameleon—
A reptile with its infinite disguises.

I beckon you on with the promise
Of an escape to safety . . .

But my arms soon transform
Again to vines I slip round your body,
Hold you; heave air from your lungs.
I tighten them, hard until your shouts
Are wheezes, desperate last breathes.
When you are silent

I exhume your body
From your sandy grave.
Air and grit splutters from your swollen lips.
I drag your remains among the palms
Where I remake myself a tiger
By the red light of the midnight moon.

The Spell

Liam Garriock

(from a painting by Sir William Fettes Douglas)

In their study, the lone necromancers
    Draw arcanic symbols on the stone walls.
    Buried spirits must answer the calls
Of the necromancers, who seek answers
From the unearthed skull. What is the future
    Of the king and the queen, of the kingdom?
    What glory awaits, what forces shall come?
What fate shall the kingdom have to endure . . . ?

The wraith appears ere the staid magicians.
    The question is asked, the answer is told. . . .
       Outside, the kingdom is shrouded in twilight.
The ghoulish wraith departs, and a great cold
    Chills the fearful men. Soon all ambitions
       Will be lost into the ultimate Night.

Moonlight in the Playground

Christina Sng

We wander the quiet playground
Hand-in-hand, chain-linked
And bound, blood thick within blood.

The moon is ivory rich tonight,
Shrouded by grey cotton wool clouds
Casting a soft filter on the foggy night.

My little girl softly hums
A bedtime melody about
Dragons and warrior children.

We pass by elephant swings
And an octopus roundabout,
And then she spies it,

Lets go of my hand,
Racing lightspeed toward it,
The dragon of her dreams:

Spiral loops wound in the air;
Musical notes crescendoing
Into a grand finale—

A dragon-headed slide, where
The little one now glides down,
Laughing with sheer joy,

My sweet soprano;
The high notes on
A child's piano.

My boy is swinging
Upside down from
One of the spirals;

My bass clef, arms now
Outstretched, reminding me
Of those dexterous acrobats

We saw on television last week.
When did he let go
Of my hand to go play?

My focus has lost its razor
These days. Perhaps it is truly
Time to rest and hibernate.

The clouds yawn, puffing apart
To reveal a luminously silver moon.
She brightens up the entire night sky.

I call to them softly, kiss
Their disappointed cheeks,
Remind them that

Even the best orchestras
Need to end; and all living
Things need to sleep.

They nod in acquiescence,
Pondering now what wondrous
Adventures their dreams will bring.

And so I begin to sing,
An old melody my mother
Taught me as a child.

I hold their hands tight,
Feel our shared blood
Pulse between us.

Slowly we fade to star dust,
Drifting back into the skies,
Into the mysterious universe

Where we belong.

An Unimaginable Horror

Norbert Gora

Apocalypse didn't start
with red clouds
and twisted branches
of green bolts

the end showed its face
accompanied by painful groans
piercing the sky
irritating sounds of the dead's orchestra

musical chords out of this world
butchered the senses like beasts
with flower of a primitive instinct
growing in the hearts
a man has become a wolf
hungry for someone else's blood

an unimaginable horror
spread its filthy limbs
and appropriated the land
bathed in respect and love

brother bit his brother
sister took the soul of her mother
scarlet paths messed each pavement up
a picture of pain and despair

The Fugitives

Manuel Pérez-Campos

Curious orchard of ensorceled men,
ye who toward your duties were remiss
that ye might enter the old acropolis
and reap there the ray of the ascended sun's
absence: Now ye, rejects of all nations,
cannot undo the torque of thy paralysis—
nor, by denying the soil of this abyss,
recover the hauteur of thy erstwhile ken.

Ye are tame ranks now, rooted in the seasons,
condemned to yield thy fruits to infidel
hands and swarmed by locusts which bowdlerize
thy sense of as yet unrevealèd crowns
Aye, gnawed by the nightmare agonies of hell
and even death oblivious to thy cries.

Under the Tuscan Moon

Leigh Blackmore

(for Elizabeth Barrett Browning)

With portraits in black carven antique frames
And chambers quaint and curiously wrought
I dwell unearthly; all Pennini's games
Have failed to cheer; my sweet child's kiss is naught.

Nathaniel Hawthorne and his wife a-stroll
Have come to call; but this is not enough
Distraction for my burning, passionate soul;
The flimsy fabric of such mundane stuff

Holds not my interest; lost in idle song,
Even my husband plays as much as works.
For me, I must have fervour, blended strong,
Suffused with Spirit for my rhymes, else lurks

The threat of ennui 'neath midsummer skies,
The sinking down beneath the brooding wings
Of coming Death; this haven yet I prize
For bringing time to pen my offerings—

To summits rising on celestial planes;
To scarlet roses, as to lilies white;
To colours in the shadows. For my pains,
Hell's vespers, prayed in ink, illume the night.

As golden orb of day—irradiate
With ordinary matters—now gives way,
Life darkens into dusk. I leave my mate;
My lines live on; I live but for today.

Kappa Alpha Tau

Josh Medsker

We have heard of the couple
torturing our kind. Tonight we
strike, brothers and sisters.

We creep on soft feet, approach,
corner, avenge. We feast, and clean
their bones.

Yes, There Are Wonders Beyond Death

Darrell Schweitzer

Yes, there are wonders beyond death:
armies that have never known the living world or the sun
marching across landscapes that stretch on forever like dark dreams,
lakes of frozen fire, forests of bone
that bleed and scream at the slightest tremor,
impossible cities and castles high in the basalt mountains,
where strange ships crewed by demons descend from a black moon
to barter jewels for slaves and souls;
the skies filled with thunderous wings
while prophets atop peaks and towers
babble of what was, is, and is to come,
proclaiming the termination of mankind,
while behind the mountains, behind the black moon,
amid the burnt-out cinders of stars, the gods themselves
stand helpless and blank-faced, and the universe itself
dissolves into fine, chaotic dust, to swirl before the throne of Azathoth.

rUBBLE ®ubbLe

Jason V Brock

—saVage dreaming;

Y4WNING ink-black-s0ul-ch1mes . . . .

~Cassilda! *Cassilda!*~   A:

Match Ed nothing   which darkly shines, pines,

LINES. Of. Cove(r)ted. Beauty.

Chaotic wonder divined? The no answer, is

"YES . . ."

[chorus]

rUBBLE ®ubbLe

You FACEless mess!

rUBBLE ®ubbLe

yOU've torn your   breast;

rUBBLE ®ubbLe

LqqK . . . below!

King's rob3s

My beLov ED is yellow'd SO!

It is (k)nown, The PLAY'S the Thing—

With the Hammett-chiseled wonderfolliclesRiff-sHotGun . . .

BEmuSe theyMUSE of the aMused

"Be NOT! Beware, despair—*au contraire.*"

. . . Piano wIRE G4RROTE blasted heath deceit . . .
¡Beast—
Veils of *dun* chartreuse . . .   [in]sidious haute h(u)e(s)? ¿Are you BoY
or gIRl?

/SCREAMS!/ SCREams . . ./

[chorus]
                    rUBBLE ®ubbLe
                                You FACEless mess!
                    rUBBLE ®ubbLe
yOU've torn your   breast;
                    rUBBLE ®ubbLe

LqqK . . . below!
King's rob3s

                            My beLov ED is yellow'd SO!

Desolation

M. F. Webb

Gray dust: parched of all nurturing, and proud
Of spines and thorns, and blossoms that reveal
Themselves but twice a year, then burn to shrouds.
Stone. Oil stains. Barbed wire. None left to feel

Or speak, save those too long to sand inclined.
As if no other world breathed past these skies,
And desecrated desert's sulfured rind
Could feed the soul and nullify its cries.

Befouled night that with emphatic claws
Threatens to decant the marrowed bone
Now stalks a home that never solace was
With horror set as its foundation stone

Till all vitality is trapped and caught
And nothing red beats in the blighted dusk.
Flesh burns to sand, and cindered blood is naught
But residue. My arid heart: dried husk.

The Cosmic Women

Pat Calhoun

Where are the cosmic women? for they must be;
To find them is my destiny.
They taunt me with glimpses in the sultry sky;
Stars festoon their hair as they fly.

They sing a song that fills the void with longing
For the bliss they keep promising
With comet-tipped breasts and galaxy-rich thighs.
But dark stars that shine in their eyes

Hint that all their love may be lies, a deadly
Disguise they wear to lure their prey.
For I feel the last of this worshiper's soul
Now consumed, leaving a black hole.

Descent

Ian Futter

Born in a cradle of burning stars,
where free-falling fires
slash the bright sky
with scars.

Scars like the mark
etched into my skull,
where the steady hand slipped,
scoring deep the womb's hull.

Or the gash that I felt
from a friendship's first flight;
all the brightness burnt out
to dead rocks in the night,

or the slits and the slicing
from the scythe of time's power,
as he hastens my drop
from eternity's tower.

Always the falling,
but never to land,
I must flash through this life;
a brief light trail, unplanned.

Then someone; a voice,
speaking light through the black,
calmly stifles my blaze
and puts all the stars back.

The God-Builders

Nathaniel Reed

Vain humanity grasps with calloused fingers
at boundless corridors beyond the rim of earth,
but what is to be seized upon in the loneliness
between the reach of stars?
Miserably alone, they conjure forth new images
from the dust of the once fearsome earth,
titan forms that coalesce and turn their visage
downward onto their mortal architects.

Sated on their sacrilege, the god-builders
gaze upon those avatars in revelry,
yet how the whole of the earth soon trembles
beneath the cataclysm of their ascent!
The countenance of behemoths betrays
neither joy nor pity amid tumultuous creation.
Their hands bestow not the bounty of blessing,
but answer infirmity with insurmountable wrath.

And in their coming, the world shall be delivered
unto a mausoleum horrific in its endless dimension . . .

Sighting

Ross Balcom

alone
in attic

or garage
you might see it

your shadow
self

the one
you shouldn't see

standing there
blazing

voiceless, black
a midnight flame

Falling for You

John J. Mundy

Will we recognize Its smile
when It comes to us;
Its dark and gaping maw
filled with the soundless mirth
of freshly turned earth?
                    —The Abyss

"I distrust smiles," he said to her.

"Really?" said the pretty girl. "Wouldn't the world be a sad place without smiles?"

"I can't help it," he said. "Ever since childhood I've felt that way. Why, even the most genuine ones seem false to me. I dread what might be behind them . . . hiding perhaps. Or waiting. Something evil and hideous."

The lights and sounds of the party were already far behind them.

"Well, then," said his pretty companion, linking her arm in his. "I'll simply never smile at you again. Would you like that?"

The conversation had become awkward. He had drunk too much. And making such confessions was not readily in his nature.

"Why, no," he said. "No, I wouldn't . . . I think you have a wonderful smile."

"Then I'm glad," she said, suddenly, teasingly, pulling away, clapping her hands with the enthusiasm of a happy child.

A moment passed and she spoke once more, very somberly this time.

"You are wrong you know . . . about smiles."

"Yes," he agreed, "of course I am." His head was slightly spinning as they walked in the cool evening air. "It's all foolishness I know but I can't help it."

She frowned at him. A very pretty frown.

"I didn't mean that, *silly*," she said. "I mean you're *wrong* about smiles. It's *faces* that are horrible."

And laughing merrily she peeled the flesh of her face slowly off, revealing the glistening and hungry Blackness inside.

The world spun madly about him as into her starless Dark he fell . . . screaming . . .

Somehow, in that moment, he sensed she was still smiling prettily.

Icons

Ronald Terry

Icon of god,
the head of Vlad Tepes
gazes west
from the walls of Byzantium.

Rain links earth to sky.
Voices awaken,
impaled upon lightning spikes,
singing their pain
into painted darkness.

Blood flows through
the portal of bones
to feed the lives
of eternal ghosts.

No one knows
what the rising sun will display.
But martyrs dance
beneath domed roofs,
freed from beliefs
that tortured their lives
and constructed their deaths.

The Sword

Chad Hensley

In my pale hand, a great white sword appears.
I tremble: power vast at my command,
Imbued with might beyond the outer spheres
And knowledge weird that this has all been planned.

A mouth grins wide from hilt in platinum blade.
With grimace, metal lips shout daemon name
With utter alien voice, fears simply fade.
Around the sword springs magic, fulgent flame.

The sword now screams; forthwith I disappear
With loud blue burst of hissing electricity.
Atop the spine tower, I instantly appear
Armed with helm and sword; such simplicity.

I shout at massing daemon hordes below.
Lift the new blade high as it screams with woe.

Dual Purpose

Kyla Lee Ward

A lantern casts a shadow in the day
and little things of darkness fight for room
where iron fretwork turns the sun away
and bull's eye panels cast a spectral bloom.
Such demons as are sloughed like ash from Hell,
and lost familiars, waiting witch's prayer.
Glimpse fledgling gargoyles, yet to grow a shell,
and spirits trapped in necromantic snare.
As men may huddle in a shaft of light
as twilight drowns the square and meeting hall,
so many of the haunts that give them fright
cling writhing there, until the night shall fall.
And when the glass at last begins to heat,
a wave of terror rushes up the street.

A Dream from R'lyeh

Charles Lovecraft

At first it seemed just like a dream. It had
The shape and texture of a dream, with beams
Mere nothingness provides that yet exude
A vast suggestiveness, and cryptic streams
Of an impossible kind of strange life
That made one feel it wasn't real. But then
It would not go away, and its deep strife
Just carved much deeper in the shuddering ken.

And then it was just like a knife revealed
That severed all the threads of disbelief
And my poor brain, engulfed in awe, just reeled,
Poised on that world . . . came to life . . . bas-relief . . .
Something too large for words, fiendish and close—
The streaming realm whole atmospheres across.

The Witch of the Woods

Frank Coffman

A tale among the Slavic races:
An old witch dwells deep in the wood.
Their folklore teems with hints and traces
Of a wicked crone scarce understood.
She rides a mortar, wields a pestle—
Gliding about in that strange vessel,
She haunts the depths of children's dreams
And nightmares deathly dark. It seems
Some think that she can bring a blessing;
To others she's a bane, a curse,
A glimpse of Hell, or even worse—
Even great sinners start confessing
When of the wicked old one hear
Or think the Baba Yaga's near.

Fallen

Claire Smith

The seeds will bring your town
Good luck forever for just a halfpenny
I promise you boy.
They'll have you back, you wait!
The rag and bone man will help—
He does his sums quick—
Less than the cost of the apples he stole.

The boy throws the seeds on some scrub:
Bushes germinate, sprout and grow.
They'll get so big folk will never starve!
The old man's words echo . . .
They'll forget your crimes
They'll all be history.
But when the rains come,

Winds blow, and on hot days
The honey from the blossoms
Pulls the animals too close
With their magnetic sweetness—
So close they're bound to the bushes.
Poison thorns soon grow
And the white flowers drip

The Devil's blood.
The sheep, pigs, and cows;
Chickens as well, are left to die.
Mauled by barbs,
Attached to the sharp hedge . . .
Rotten, stuck fast as if to rusted metal
Smoke drowns out the once bright sky.

The Germ of the Earth

Farah Rose Smith

We are but the germ of the earth
No jungle nor city may purge—
A capture of seething carnage,
Amass on the ire of man—
Wavering not by the bay,
Or any sea swept above the abyss—
Clan by clan crept to the quiet dune,
And were met by the shivering sands—
Broadly, the night carried over—
The last of the sun was in view—
Each eye was limitlessly older,
Glazed by the right tarnished hand—
The weeds began wilting again—
At last, when the choir sound grew,
Amass on the ire of man,
The light of the sky split in two—
No faith nor fervor may urge,
For we are but the germ of the earth.

The Road to Long-Ago

Ruth Berman

Pumpkin moon heavy in the sky—
Clouds broom-thin riding the wind—
Brown leaves blowing
On the halloweenshadow street—

Show ghosts the way
To yesterday

The road to Long-ago.

Spawn of the Wicked Hive

Jeff Burnett

These ghastly things that men call cities fair,
These vermin pits, these vile contagion pools—
Damn these wicked hives veneered in jewels
Where jackals scumber in the market square,
Where honor dies within the viper's lair,
And sewer grates scab with filth and human ooze;
Upon the temple steps the dung accrues:
Avarice becomes the sacred prayer.

A hydra black with pestilential foam,
A maze of rats submerged in venomed slime,
This foul miasma spawns a species weak,
Lost within unwholesome pantomime:
Decrepit creatures bent before a throne—
Fitting fodder for the vulture's beak.

Night Play

Ashley Dioses

So innocent and timeless, wild and rare,
Pegasus was a wonder to behold.
I saw him once, out dancing in the cold
Beneath the stars, and soaring through the air.
He caught my eyes and stopped to match my stare.
His prideful eyes had glowed like molten gold
When lightning struck, yet still I stood, so bold.
He tempted me to then approach, to dare. . . .

He sprang into the air to soar and glide
Amid the boundless kingdoms of the sky,
And galloped through the graying clouds with pride.
He proudly pranced, displaying for my eyes
His majesty as master of the night—
Yet ere the dawn, he left my tearful sight.

The Prey

Mary Krawczak Wilson

Always the eyes of the iconic owl
Seek out the spilt blood
After the venomous flood
To lacerate its prey so foul.

Appearing in shadows, the vulture
Vacillates like a trapeze artist in its cave,
Awaiting the voluminous waves
To spit its prey into an abyssal culture.

Awash in a scarlet sea, the crustacean
Crawls toward its barnacled tomb
Poised, proud, and ready to assume
Its prey in an otherworldly station.

Blending into the desert inferno, the snake
Captures its prey and gyrates in a pyrrhic
Dance to the sun—stark and sulfuric
As its victim's bones crumble and break.

A Return

Benjamin Blake

The sound travels furthest at night.
Over empty fields, and lonely farm houses.
The flap of leathery wings
forewarns of my return.

This coastal city knows my name.
Though they dare only speak in hushed whispers
Born at the unholy hour,
one midwinter night
many years ago

The old stone church now sits boarded up.
The nave gathering dust.
But there are always new maidens.
I shall drink of their blood.
The one from my homelands,
stripped bare beneath the cold stars.
Waxen skin bathed in the moon's soft glow.
She will be found come morning.
Laid out like so many before her.
Though, if fortuitous, she will wake,
when the sun sinks in fallow ground,
blessed with this eternal curse.

When the Earth Was Young

Christina Sng

When the Earth was young,
She was engulfed in fire.

Her seas brimmed
With crimson lava,

Her skies painted
In black opal.

Volcanic mountains
Filled the horizon,

And the world
Was ruled by dragons.

Above,
They soared,

Magnificent ruby kites,
High in the charcoal skies,

Until the day
The first asteroids fell

And began
Earth's Age of Ice.

The House of Gloom

Adam Bolivar

I tell of Jack, who blew the horn
To wake the giant in the morn,
Whose clothes are old and tattertorn,
Who seeks Yᵉ Tower in the thorn.

He left the inn, Yᵉ Toad and Crow,
    His countenance forlorn,
For he had nothing left to blow
    Now that he'd lost his horn.

Jack journeyed onward down the road,
    In hopes his fortune turned;
A vision to him was bestowed,
    Since childhood had it burned:

Within a Tower's garret wait
    A Lady with a Cup;
But first Jack had to pass the gate
    Before he could climb up.

He heard an owl's hoot in the day—
    An omen to be sure;
Jack felt that he had lost his way,
    His heart become impure.

The thorn-hemmed path wound on and on;
    Jack slowly down it crept;
The hell-mouth opened in a yawn,
    While angels softly wept.

He found himself in yellow'd reed,
    A marshy, mazy place,
A place a rampant hare would lead
    If any give him chase.

Beyond the reed there lay a pond,
    Where willows swayed and bent,
Where frogs in legions came to spawn,
    Where lilies wafted scent.

Beside the pond, a rain-worn stone
    In which was carved the name
Of Mary who once sat alone,
    And dreamt she played a game.

Beyond the pond a marble tomb,
    A hoary crumbling vault;
Who lay inside had met their doom—
    This insight made Jack halt.

Quietus came for all one day,
    But would not come for him,
For Jack was favoured by the fey,
    Enduring at their whim.

I do not mean this mortal coil,
    For Jack like all must die,
But underneath the fertile soil,
    He never long would lie.

His spirit was a blazing fire,
    Called Jakkios of old;
By nature he would never tire
    Of hearing Jack-tales told.

Jack cheated death and was reborn,
    A baby, squalling, new;
And when he came of age a horn
    A purpose would imbue.

Then from the tomb Jack turned away;
    The charnel stench was vile;
The noxious odour of decay
    Did little to beguile.

Before him loomed Old Ettinfell,
    The fallen house of Drake,
Whose souls abode in darkest hell
    Till Golden Dawn a-break.

Jack strode up to the rotting door,
    Of once-stout oaken beams;
The ancient arms of Drake loomed o'er,
    A wyrm from fitful dreams.

Well, who should open up that door
    But long-eared Harold Gloom?
Jack stepped upon the creaking floor,
    Which echoed like a tomb.

"The House of Drake is now of Gloom,"
    Then Harold smugly said.
"The last Drake willed it with a plume
    Before collapsing dead."

His tenure Jack did not protest,
    Or call the hare a cheat;
He only asked a place to rest,
    And for a bite to eat.

Begrudgingly, Gloom played the host
 And fed Jack in the hall
A crust of bread without a roast,
 And even that was small.

And then he took Jack to a room,
 Its furnishings austere;
Such was the welcome of the Gloom,
 A courtesy most queer.

But when the hour of witches chimed,
 Jack crept out of his room,
And up the stairs he softly climbed,
 Neglected by the broom.

Jack opened up the attic door
 By turning thrice the key;
He'd learned this secret scrap of lore
 Upon his beldam's knee.

He felt he had been here before,
 Inside this attic room,
And so he entered it once more,
 Atop the House of Gloom.

Upon the writing desk a book,
    Embossed a cruel design:
A horned black shepherd with a crook—
    It was Y^e Crimsonne Sygne.

Well, Jack the game would not give up;
    He played his final card:
Y^e Lady waiting with Y^e Cup,
    Whose path and Jack's were starred.

The seven-angled sign he drew
    Upon a virgin page;
The magick from his fingers flew,
    A skilled and potent mage,

For Jack had something Harold lacked:
    The ancient blood of Drake;
He spilt a drop and by that act,
    Winged Dumah stirred awake.

Y^e Angel carried Jack aloft
    Into a barren land,
And like a feather landed soft
    Upon the shifting sand.

Y^e Tower loomed, so dark and old;
    Jack stormed up to the gate,
His blood was stirring, hot and bold,
    Athirst to meet his fate.

Y^e Silver Key he jammed and turned
    Inside the iron lock;
His efforts, though, the tumblers spurned—
    The gate, a fractious block.

And then it dawned. Alas! Alack!
    He had no horn to blow.
Y^e Tower faded into black,
    While starkly laughed a crow.

Once more in Darkened Wood Jack was,
    Beside a trickling stream,
Snatched from Abaddon's hungry jaws,
    Y^e Tower but a dream.

Elder Beings

Leigh Blackmore

They came across abysses from doomed planes
Unutterably distant, far from ken
Of human beings writhing in their pain
Of mortal life—mere women and mere men.

They fled their crumbling towers and citadels
In search of living planets for their use
And so Alhazred's secret mad book tells
They flocked and settled on the Earth, let loose

To rave and raven. Human minds succumbed
To alien thought-forms of these Elder Things.
Through fevered dreams their dreadful visions thrummed,
These creatures with their terrible black wings.

And so at last it was that humankind
Obliterated, lived and thrived no more.
The Elder Beings in their might combined
Had shattered human life—so tells the lore!

Reunion

Manuel Pérez-Campos

We, the undead, who limp while hillsides sleep,
past the elms' shrunk shadows, past the pasture's
tenure, past the burnt-out lampposts' allures,
and past the bleak lawns of your dead end street,
are coming for you through this wee hour's heat.
We whose figures the stained cloud sky obscures,
out of church soil and out of dull dank sewers:
It is for you, brother, that we moan and creep.

And while you're nude and whistling, we'll be drooling
past your backyard's porch door at a shuffling pace,
then past the hall above the staircase landing—
thick-girthed some of us, but most of us still thin—
snarling, bumping, creaking, until we reach in-
side your shower and touch your crumpling face.

The Awen

Michelle Claire White

I am the light that lifts the heart
To realms of poetry and art,
Illuminating truth and song
That was within you all along;
And in your belly I am fire,
Sweet unfurling wild desire,
Raging, burning, bright and strong,
Becoming firestorm of song.

Open to me if you dare
To sing, to speak, to make, to care.

What now will you dare to dream?
What sights have only your eyes seen?
What tale is sweet upon your tongue,
What wild dance is not yet done?
Pen to paper, foot to floor,
Pain to canvas—go, explore!
By bleeding hearts and sweating pores
I am the Awen, I am yours.
By pounding heart and beating drum,
I am the Awen, I have come.

The Awen is a force for change,
For inspiration sweet and strange
To cleanse the heart and fire the mind
And balm the soul of humankind.

By pounding heart and beating drum,
I am the Awen, I have come.

I am the tonic and the mead
Of artists' blood and poets' seed;
The flowing water of the muse
More sweet than any mortal booze.
Drink deep of me and you will find
Your voice, your song I will unbind,
Your hands untie, your toes uncurl,
Your art burst free upon the world.

By pounding heart and beating drum,
I am the Awen, I have come.

Ghosts of 1816

Clay F. Johnson

> "My imagination, unbidden, possessed and guided me . . . I saw the hideous phantasm . . . and I wished to exchange this ghastly image of my fancy for the realities around . . . the dark parquet . . . the moonlight struggling through, and the sense I had that the glassy lake and white high Alps were beyond. I could not so easily get rid of my hideous phantom; still it haunted me."
>
> —Mary Shelley, Introduction to *Frankenstein* (1831 edition)

Deathlike beneath the cold ray of the moon
Bathing in its sinful silver-white shine;
Enshadowed in the distance as my gloom-
Teased eyes glean over one last sanguine line,
Reading by moonlight in wickedness divine.
Teeming now with thoughts that God may impugn,
I pour the perfumed peridot,
And set imagination loose
In the opalescent louche,
Raising the unhallowed arts in poetic woe.

The sky told a story that haunted me
As the galvanized air lit up with light;
It was a tempest meant so fittingly
To raise Death's shadowy forms of delight.
And yet who could say that this dreary night
Did not console the ghost-gleamed literati?
The livid hues and shades of death

Inspired the spark of creation,
Infusing life with re-animation
To thick my lab-maddened blood with its stifled breath.

My dark imagination murmurs in
Subtle numbness, a drowsy sense among
Sour smells writhed in softened yellow-grey skin
As moaning escaped its mold-flowered tongue—
To the galvanometer I now clung,
Watching its death-plucked eyes and wrinkled grin.
The drops of the ice-cold drip
Releases the ethereal spirits,
Creating dew-frosted ringlets
From a pontarlier I now lovingly sip.

As I drink I think of Ariel sails,
Sleepless gossamers toward my blonde-haired harlot;
Her cerulean blue eyes bring back tales
Of her sinister-sweet lips, dark scarlet,
Made for the tear-soaked attic of my Gothic Charlotte.
The poetry of swirling herbal trails
Presage my dark seduction:
The green anise that did benumb
My tongue as a bitter drop of laudanum
Brought forth my faery-borne glitter-eyed abduction.

Suddenly, in a conscious memory,
Solemn, serene, in mysteriousness
I gazed upon the ice of Chamonix;
Cheating despair in moonless wilderness,
Musing and anxious in the calm darkness
Upon the peak in awful majesty.
Discovering undiscovered solitudes
On this wind-swept edge—one more step, never,
Yet I wished to fall, and fall forever
Through swift vapors in Nature's breathless altitudes.

Dark vibrant colors begin to take me,
Jade and emerald gems, light golden hues,
Fragrant oils released, death-white and ghostly,
With blood reds, Veronese greens and lush blues—
An aesthetic paleness in herbal dews
Stirs the madness in chilling melody.
The licorice sweetness I crave
Of delirium and nightmares,
Beckoning for other-worldly cares
From the enviable qualities of the grave.

This elixir of life brings back my ghosts
To roam freely in imagination;
Visions of the spectre-barked dead that toasts
To solemn delights of putrefaction
As breasts with eyes watch with satisfaction.
Bitter wormwood, its herbaceous taste boasts
Of what its poison does to a sweet face,
Twisting in Nature's poetic madness,
Brooding over Her loveliness
That the sallow effects of Death will one day grace.

Quetzalcoatl

Kendall Evans

Lord of the Star of Dawn
Winged Quetzalcoatl
Broods above volcanoes
Soars on hot-ash updrafts
Plumed serpent
Take up your sacrifice
Of birds & snakes
Be merciful
Withhold the Winds of Wrath
Bring gentle breezes
Quetzalcoatl
Creator of man
Did you foresee the end
Years never calendared
Quietly concluding?
Are you and your sibling Gods
Extinct
As old volcanoes?
Or are you fuming forever
Quetzalcoatl
In glowing hot magma
Flowing deep beneath our feet
Our cities, our superhighways

Quetzalcoatl
Do you shake the stars?
Are the Pleiades
Your serpent's rattle?

Relic

Nathaniel Reed

creaking walls barely held against the wrathful wind
a roof buckled under the agonizing weight of winter
windows blinded by a generation of unwashed dust

how that house has stood for a century undisturbed
on the farthest road lost in the shade of evergreens

a relic even among the ancient giants spreading to realms
marked only by fallen needles rotting languidly

a lonely wretch at the edge of an apathetic world
insignificant like the ghosts who walk its halls

Admonishments for the Incautious

David Barker

To spare thee horrific fright
when languishing souls
emerge from tree boles,
stay away from all windows at night.

So as not to provoke the undead,
do not venture deep down
into crypts below ground—
thou art better off snug in thy bed.

Yet fiends enter dreams without leave,
and cause massive alarm
as they inflict great harm:
interlopers who will lie and deceive.

A door that's locked four times is safe,
while bolted thrice is a curse,
and done six fold is worse—
even numbers bar midnight's vile waif.

To be brave is no feat in the light,
yet when day has departed
even bold men stout-hearted
Know spirits go marauding at night.

Yaga

Oliver Smith

Mother Maggot lives in the house
Of the sun: her deathly deathless,
Living lifeless, skinny skinless
Face worn down to a half-moon skull
By ravens, worms, and summer rain.
Mother Maggot's lonely cottage
Built of bones in the deep wood
Among the green oaks and orchids
Where the hangman's bloody gibbets stood.

Down a path of thornapple, hemlock,
And flowers of bitter rue. You might
Meet the darkness of her empty eye;
Or see her gory grinning teeth
Smiling in the coiling ivy
Knotted over stone finials
And half eroded gargoyles.
Mother Maggot in a coat of goatskin,
Kidskin, childskin. On her yellow flesh

A dress of rags like scarlet rowan.
The hag hides among the rose hips,
Hedgerow apples, violet bullace.
She's waiting in the house of the sun:
Deathly deathless, living lifeless,
Skinny skinless half-moon skull.

Her thrush-bone pen writes
Over windows "remember me"
As she brews her dreams from henbane,

Wolfbane, nightshade, and agrimony.
Remember before oblivion and darkness
Submerge her sunset memory.
Time has chewed this widow
Down to footsteps in silk-dressed
Shadows among burrs and thistles.
A curse whispered in the brambles.
A poem splattered on the road
In the blood of broken berries.

In the thorns her eye glimmers
With a malignant irritation.
There's the pool of black water
Among hollow oaks
Where the yellow frog croaks.
In the shallows Mother Maggot floats
Her empty face waiting
Deathly deathless, living lifeless
Skinny skinless: unreflected.

The Demon Corn

D. L. Myers

All stained with the bloody light of sunset,
The crimson stalks shake and snap in the wind.
The bare field before them glows like a lake of fire
And on its shore the dead corn dances.
Its rasping voice calls to the ruddy moon
That bulges above the forest cloaked hills,
A sentinel of the endless, black ocean of night.
And as the stars cascade and swirl across the sky,
The stalks wither in shadows
Until they are black and crisp in the night wind.

Timeless Ghosts

Liam Garriock

My eyes are clouded with the endless sights
That plague me all my days and all my nights.
I live alone, but *They* always haunt me,
Shadows and forms that will not leave me be.
From the folds of Time they ride, horses, hounds,
Racing across the skies; the mighty sounds
Of galloping and baying fill the sky
As the phantom beasts and riders pass by.
Kings of the elves, of the dead, King Arthur,
All ride through the skies, from the sepulchre,
To lonely fields, to the desolate sea.
I see them, riding above a city
Of glass, and rusted metal, and concrete,
Where rotted corpses litter every street.
A great ruin of the future, war-torn
And devastated, cold, standing forlorn
Against the ashen skies; and the phantom
Procession rides above this dead kingdom.
Wraiths of kings mourn the thousands departed.
Austere, mounted Odin, sombre-hearted,
Rides on, leaving the icy, blasted shell
To decay in its wintry, haunted hell.

Clearing Sky

Ronald Terry

One of the stars above
is my alter ego.
I forgot its name,
if I ever knew it.

I see it by its song,
a windy thought
on a rainy night.

Everything is damp
and playing dead,
strengthening itself
for the real day
the stars in the sky
close their eyes.

The Door

Christina Sng

Darkening winter
a crow entangled
in branches

Race for
the fastest ships
drowning man

Crossed line
forgiveness
an impossibility

Red fire
even a spider
has something to fear

Street performance
a girl cannot escape
herself

Incurable disease
even the queen
has no power over it

Summer's end
an old friend
holds the door

Tending the Grave

Ian Futter

So strange; we mow
above the dead,
the grass that tops
the soil-sealed head.

Where every blade,
that reaches on,
reminds us of
a loved one gone.

And every cut,
so clean and neat;
the brutal blow
of death, replete.

So harsh this severed
plane of green,
that crowns the case
of bones, unseen,

where framed, in
drying drops of dew,
my maudlin eye
bends time to view

those moments in
the pulse-gripped beat,
where life and loss
are prone to meet.

Woodsmoke: A Folk Song That Never Was

John Shirley

Her face appeared within the smoke,
—she'd died that very day—
She said, "You are alone and broke:
but there is another way."

Smoke and fire formed her face,
pine smoke her deep brown hair;
rising sparks became her eyes,
and her gown was rippling air.

> *"There might be a little hope my dove—*
> *a flash of light breaks through—*
> *there might be a wisp of hope my love,*
> *that drifts between us two!"*

As night wore on she drifted still,
the coals her lips of fire;
she blew a kiss like a nightbird's trill
—'twas from her funeral pyre.

All they had for a wedding ring
was a twist or two of smoke;
"But bells of shining ice will sing—
if you cast away your cloak."

"There might be a little hope my dove—
a flash of light breaks through—
there might be a wisp of hope my love,
that drifts between us two!"

"If you lay still this frigid night
and let the fire die down—
by morning we will drift the heights
far from this shanty town . . ."

His brother found his icy form
beside the ashen pyre;
his frozen gaze fixed on the sky—
where smoky shapes rose higher . . .

"There might be a little hope my dove—
a flash of light breaks through—
there might be a wisp of hope my love,
that drifts between us two!"

The Wolf's Last Words

Claire Smith

I'd chosen every haunted noise:
Loud, shrill at times, then soft;
Low or high tones.
I fitted them to your moods—
Like snug gold slippers transformed to snakes
Tied round they strangled your feet
So your veins wept violet.
You with your crimson cloak, hooded;
It still reeked of forests long ago cut down.

All the better to bathe you in;
All the better to shred its velour cloth;
All the better to expose your scarred skin.

Bloody murderous woman
I've fought and gained victory of sorts—
Your mind became my toy.
I threw it down a well full of snakes
They wrapped round it, choked, suffocated
Until you couldn't think straight.
You became a dazed old maid,
Walked the town's twilit streets,
Stared blank toward Heaven.

All the better to drive you mad;
All the better to feed you to the snakes;
All the better to defeat you with bear claws.

My fur coat was made into a rough cut rug
Slap-dashed on your parents' pantry stone slabs.
Your father has been dead years:
My voices turned his warnings to a whisper of doom,
My voices dulled his lamp's comforting shine,
My voices charmed you from his musical cocoon.
I've been released from my limbo with images—
I saw your body fall, float and drift downstream
Alien grey face; and plaits tied with the river's reeds.

All the better to scratch out your sanity;
All the better to deliver your eulogy;
All the better when you were coupled with death.

Dark Solstice Cold and Deathly

Richard L. Tierney

You folk who dwell in balmy austral parts
    Can never know the chill of boreal cold
    When the Frost Giants waken, grim and bold,
And Ymir's icy claws clutch round your hearts.

Earth's axis tips, the polar vortex grows
    As wakening Giants of eternal frost
    Stride south with howling ice-winds to accost
The towns, enshrouding them 'neath smothering snows.

The townsfolk cringe to sense the gusting breath
    Of Ithaqua, Great Old One of the North.
    Crouched by their hearths, they fear to venture forth,
Knowing those howling gusts are winds of death.

The winter solstice brings no Christmas cheer,
    Only the longest night and shortest day.
    Outside, the Wendigo stalks down its prey
While in their houses mortals quake in fear.

Forbear, O austral folk, to venture forth
    From your midsummer comforts so benign
    And brave those boreal latitudes malign
Where howl the icy death-winds of the north.

The Rainy Season

John J. Mundy

From somewhere a Spanish guitar
Is strummed slowly,
Falteringly, imperfectly,
Drifting over the sounds of animals—
Horses, dogs, hens.
You ignore them all.
They mean nothing to you now.

You mount the worn wooden steps
Hands chained behind your back.
Your eyes mad and defiant;
You think of a wife and child.
Your steel resolve seems less sure.
The rope feels rough against your neck;
It is quickly tightened; the chains
Replaced by more coarse rope.
Finally, your legs are unshackled.
With fear and disbelief, you confront
The honeyed light of the last morning,
The morning of your plunge into darkness,
Darkness without end.
You stand unsteadily on the trap.
You can almost feel it falling away.
An unctuous official declaims the charges.
An old Padre speaks with weariness

(He's seen the death dance times before).
And carefully, decently averts his gaze
From the dampness spreading down your legs.
You'd spit on this pious fool if you could
But your mouth is dry,
Dry as dust and old bones.

But what Demon's whisper *at this fatal moment*
Inspires you to turn your gaze *outward*–
Into that mocking gathering crowd?
Your thoughts were of a woman and child
Cruelly left behind, of the bitter taste of regret
For the things you could have done . . .
Now at the rear of this angry crowd,
Standing apart from the sneers and loud curses,
You see a woman, ethereal as a vision,
With a beautiful but sorrowful face,
Clutching a crying child to her breast,
Staring forward without tears,
With a sadness so profound it maddens you.
You reel at the cruelty of this final horror:
That she should witness the agony of your death–
Your body trembles and shakes,
You cry out like a maddened animal
And you curse the Angels

And you curse your Fate
And you curse the Black Days
Of the Rainy Season
And you wish to God
You had dug their graves deeper.

Siren's Song

Ashley Dioses

O siren song, just sing to me;
Enchant my soul, for I am yours.
Just never quit your melody,
For through my beating heart it pours.

Your touch sends many strange sensations
Throughout my warm and tender core.
Who knew Hell offered such temptations
To make me ache to be so sore?

She swims the white and frigid river,
And beckons as she leads the way.
One step—I falter and I shiver;
It's then that I begin to sway.

Her dark enchantment cast a spell—
One which I cannot break to win.
Beneath her power do I dwell—
I only serve, and feed her sin.

The Mask of Leprous Light

Jeff Burnett

Aphrodite, come, dance, unearth
Evil in the eyes of blind beholders,
Malice of the moralists that moulder
In dens of filth condemning their own birth
With whips and droning chants.

Revilers of the dance and cups of mirth
Agonize in the shadow of the vulture;
Crooked spines laden with jagged boulders,
Engraved with little songs of wrath and dearth,
Grovel in blood and fright.

The eremites have shed their priestly vests,
Bedizenment, vanity, and pride
For soiled tatters purfled with ebon grime,
Thinking their blotchy hides by heaven blest,
Aglow with nimbus light.

Adorers of the carcass-worm's caress
Howl with cankered lips grim castigations;
Thralls to rituals of flagellation
Sing their canticles of plague and pest,
Rejoicing woeful plights

In arid climes, scorpion-bound, abhorred.
Condemning all with self-anointed tongues,
Noxious as the harpy's fetid dung

Slung upon the sage's feast of yore,
The desert monks of death

With sulfurous breath and senescent mouths implore
Some impotent god for abstinential grace,
For locust swarms to blight Desire's face;
They pray for purging fire, plague, and sword,
And murderous angel throngs.

Abject faith, horror, habitude
Of ragged souls demand as nutriment
Plates of pain and goblets of lament:
Holy bribes to quell the beast that broods
Within their mortal shells.

Fungous crumbs of agony the food
Of offerings rejected by the beast;
The eremites through grueling rites release
Founts of blood in the stead of Nature's dew—
Still they can't expel

The shadow of Desire from their tombs
Of scabious flesh awash in charnel stenches;
The fetor of gangrenous wounds to thwarteous senses
Semblable to musk, sweet perfume,
Bouquets of cherished rot.

The lashes wane, empurpling dusk descends;
To eventide the crepuscule gives way.
The waxing wings of Night dethrone the Day.
Mangled bodies sprawl on thorny beds
As corpse and catafalque.

Phantasmagoric visions fill their heads
As Morpheus weaves adamantean spells,
Potions drawn from Aphrodite's well:
Instinctual urges older than holy dread
Bloom like nenuphars.

In Slumber's realm no slavering tongue repents
Its burning thirst, begat by pale moonrise,
For deltas lush and wet betwixt the thighs
Of entities fantasque: their banishment
Pardoned by the stars.

Piety swept aside as spidery mesh,
Letches loosed behind the milky eye,
Lubricious as the loins of succubi,
Swell the shriveled horns of holy flesh
Throbbing in the thorns,

Long denied the velvet grip of lust.
Entanglements with nubile phantoms fair,

Both demoness and virgin, bosoms bared,
Resurrect the dead from Death's own dust,
Slither forth to sate.

Carnal gates decrepit hands unbolt
With fumbling fervor; rapaciously they prod
The nooks, the clefts, the shrines of strange new gods
Lounged on oily coils manifold,
Voluptuous, sublime:

Primeval things enswathed in serpent folds
Glistening like nymphs in silver streams.
The hermits plumb the hollows of their dreams,
Carouse as ancient kings and rutting goats,
And bow before the beast.

Again, Morpheus shall loose his grip
Upon the swirling heads and swollen horns
As merciless versicles awake the Morn:
The solar carnifex of Nyx's gifts
Strikes the gong of pain.

The crack of dawn incites the crack of whips,
Yet vestiges of nocturnal visions merge

With the striping kiss of the scarlet-dripping scourge:
Secret pleasures couched in penitence
Of skeletal eremites.

Turbid lust cocooned in righteousness:
A mask of leprous light.

Of Rippers, Psychos, and Scarves

Randall D. Larson and Charles Lovecraft

(*On Robert Bloch and Violence, a Psycho-logical approach*)

It has been said . . .
I exorcise violent tendencies thru my typewriter
This way when I see red I don't become a mad fighter
My rage infests the written page
Like Jack I live beyond my age
And with a word carpet wipe a red swath
My wrath becomes no furious psychopath
It's only in fiction where I stab the cursed blighter
Or with a shaking mitt light the igniter!
And thus it's read.

Dark Shuttle

Ruth Berman

The Shadow Weaver
Works a loom of moonbeams.
Strings of nothing
Cross the silver.

The Weaver's left
Throws the empty shuttle
At the Weaver's right
And is targeted in turn.

The shadow lengthens on the loom.

Downstream

Oliver Smith

We made sacrifices on amnesiac waters
As we drifted in search of the river's
Conclusion. We were bold adventurers,
Pleasure seekers, exiles, and ambassadors
Bound for paradise beyond the seas.
The philosopher pretended wisdom

Of the way, but no algorithm guided us:
Only rumour, only legend, only mystery.
The priest voiced some sacred theory,
And passed from clarity to unquiet dream
Afloat on dimming memory. We lay
Deep in love, deep in the dregs of sleep,

Or deep in sweet intoxicated visions.
The waters bore us far from our own land
To a place where smiling herders drove
Their flocks from lovely pasture to pleasant byres,
Summoned by bells that tolled in golden towers
To feast in the Emperor's marble palace halls.

In this happy country we sought
To make our home. We took the hands
Of youth and maid and lay among the corn,

Drinking wine pressed from the grapes
That hung so sweet and ripe and heavy
Dripping crimson from the vine.

But as nightfall spread in the azure
Of the lapidary sky, and lay like a veil
Across the gold of wheat, of flowers,
Of the scented waters, of the molten stream,
Those lovers in the asphodel, the labourers
In the field, and the emperor on the throne

All faded to palimpsests in the dusk.
Leaving us in dark and dusty grounds
Where the future crumbled in our arms
Replaced by grinning skulls and naked bones.
Our reflections: ragged skeletons who toiled
To reap the harvest of all these wasted years.

The War of Dragons

Christina Sng

Ruby skies
After the bloodletting
The dragons
Won this round

Tourmaline tunnels
Pathway to escape
The raging flames
The path to freedom

Sapphire clouds
Destroy our planes
They shatter and crumble
To the ground

Emerald mountain
Fortress without sound
The immortal ice queen
Fears eradication

As the mountains fall
And the rivers burn
Our once-fertile Earth
Seared sterile

Those who survive
Always tell the tale
Of the fruitless war
That destroyed us all

Temple of the Plumed Serpent

Ann K. Schwader

—Teotihuacán (Nahuatl): the place where men become gods

How men became gods here, or where they went,
abandoning this land for stranger skies
whose myths are sanguine miracles, defies
our scholarship. Although their monuments
depict a grim & oceanic birth,
titanic serpents, jaguars . . . all life
that means us death, we symbolize the knife
against our throats until it shatters. Earth
served only as their merest shadow-stage,
where dramas darker, deeper than our time
upon this rock replayed to realign
our destiny.   What cruel future age
of servitude awaits us may be read
in glyphs of pyrite swirling far beneath
our feet. Inside that tunnel's subtle glow,
a galaxy expands—its center dead
within a drift of mysteries, a wreath
unlike the constellations that we know.

Those

David Barker

Those dismissed as superstition
carry out a somber mission.
Just beyond life's fringe they dwell,
reaching out from deepest Hell.
Probing into lives benign,
twisting them in ways malign.

Entities defying reason
thrive in this decaying season.
Sensing the approach of Death,
they inhale each mournful breath.
Guard against these or regret
The slew of woe you thus beget.

Here beside us they reside;
by no laws do they abide.
There's a kingdom they have wrought
just beyond the edge of thought.
Ignore these specters at your peril;
From their core flows hatred feral.

Samhain Redivivus

Frank Coffman

All Hallows' Eve, the night comes round again—
Ancient *Samhain*—when spirits of the dead
Mingle with those still living ere they go
Into that realm no living man can know.
Also all manner of evils it is said—
The portals of the dark ope wide—and then
Demons and Fays, all minions of the Dark
Are free to walk the Earth on that dread night.
Still balefires blaze, the sacrifices made
To the pagan gods and goddesses of the Celt.
In hidden places are the chants still spelt,
Carved on the oak that stands nearby the glade,
Seeking to save the living from their plight.

Offerings are set, in hope to satisfy,
But animals slaughtered and the baked soulcakes
Sometimes do not appease the maddened ghosts,
Nor do they offer shelter from the hosts
Of ancient Evils. For some this dread night takes
Them right along to Hell—they too shall die.
And with the year's accumulated dead,
Shall, to that place of which no man can tell,
Go hence. To the Otherworld their spirits fly.

Samhain is pronounced "sah-ween."

Classic Reprints

The Old Ghost

Thomas Lovell Beddoes

Over the water an old ghost strode
    To a churchyard on the shore,
And over him the waters had flowed
    A thousand years or more,
And pale and wan and weary
    Looked never a sprite as he;
For it's lonely and it's dreary
    The ghost of a body to be
    That has mouldered away in the sea.

Over the billows the old ghost stepped,
    And the winds in mockery sung;
For the bodiless ghost would fain have wept
    Over the maiden that lay so young
'Mong the thistles and toadstools so hoary.
    And he begged of the waves a tear,
But they shook upwards their moonlight glory,
    And the shark looked on with a sneer
    At his yearning desire and agony.

[First published in *The Poetical Works of Thomas Lovell Beddoes*, ed. Edmund Gosse (London: J. M. Dent & Co., 1890), 77.]

Red Ghosts in Kentucky

Leah Bodine Drake

As I went home through the thirsty fields
Dark storm-clouds massed.
The heat-waves danced above the wheat
Where long ago sly doeskinned feet
Of redmen passed.

And suddenly, over Tatum's hill,
Redmen appeared!
Shawnee braves, who had made their stand
A century back in this river-land—
For a century unfeared.

Tawny-brown as the johnson-grass,
With wildcat grace
Walked the proud bucks. From war-belts swung
Scalps to which the blood still clung.
Paint masked each face.

Then I saw captives, stumbling and tied,
Herded in their wake:
Pale-faced women with babes in arms,
Grim-eyed men from the clearing-farms,
Bound for the torture-stake.

All around were the vanished trees,
Forest before, behind.
Faint cries came on the heavy air,
The brown limbs shone, the bloody hair
Rippled . . . I saw them wind

All in a bright, impossible line
Through the ghostly wood.
I watched the last plumed warrior go,
Bearing his tomahawk and bow.
Rigid I stood,

With the age-old terror awake in me
At the old name—
Shawnee!—the wolfish howls at morn,
The painted faces in the corn,
The cabin roofs aflame.

I shut my eyes and cried aloud!
Then with a roaring sound
The rainstorm broke on the fields long dry.
But was it thunder that shook the sky,
Or drums on a stamping-ground?

[First published in *Weird Tales* 44, No. 8 (January 1953): 66.]

Articles

In Pursuit of the Transcendent: The Weird Verse of Walter de la Mare

Leigh Blackmore

Walter J[ohn] Delamare—it would be thirty years before he poeticized the surname—is considered one of the most important and distinguished poets of the twentieth century and one of modern literature's chief exemplars of the romantic imagination. His complete works form a sustained treatment of romantic themes: dreams, death, rare states of mind and emotion, fantasy worlds of childhood, and the pursuit of the transcendent.

Many devotees of the macabre are at least somewhat familiar with de la Mare's work in supernatural fiction. The collection *Eight Tales* (Arkham House, 1971) features his earliest fiction, published initially under the byline of "Walter Ramal" in the *Sketch, Pall Mall Magazine,* and the *Cornhill Magazine* at the turn of the twentieth century. The tales in it foreshadow his writing of later macabre masterpieces such as "Seaton's Aunt," "All Hallows," "The Connoisseur," and "Crewe." His ghostly tales are gathered in *Ghost Stories* (Folio Society, 1936). His macabre tales, among the genre's best, appeared in such books as *The Riddle and Other Stories, The Connoisseur and Other Stories, On the Edge, A Beginning, The Wind Blows Over,* and *Collected Tales* (edited with an introduction by Edward Wagenknecht). He also wrote important fantastic novels, such as his tale of supernatural possession, *The Return.*

De la Mare's vast output includes more than forty-five volumes of work for children, mainly of fiction and poetry, but also includes essays, anthologies, and retellings of biblical stories and fairytales. Of poetry, too, he published more than forty-five volumes, ranging from *Poems* (Murray, 1906) to *The Collected Poems of Walter de la Mare* (Faber & Faber, 1979).

De la Mare's life was outwardly uneventful. He was born in 1873 and attended St. Paul's Cathedral School, his formal education not extending beyond this point. Upon graduation, he worked for the Anglo-American (Standard) Oil Company, remaining with the firm for eighteen years. He began writing short stories and poetry while working in the mundane trade of bookkeeper in the company's London office during the 1890s. His first published short story, "Kismet," appeared in the *Sketch* in 1895. In 1902, he published his first major work, the poetry collection *Songs of Childhood*, recognized as a significant example of children's literature for its creative imagery and variety of meters. The world of childhood, however, is only a facet of de la Mare's work. In 1908, following the publication of his novel *Henry Brocken* and the poetry collection titled *Poems*, de la Mare was granted a Civil List pension, enabling him to terminate his corporate employment and focus exclusively on writing. He died in 1956.

De la Mare's poems are closely linked with his stories in theme and mood, and they share with his stories ambiguous, often obscure treatment of supernatural themes. His verse is imbued with the same indefiniteness and aura of fantasy as story collections like *The Riddle and Other Stories* (1923).

Critics often assert that a childlike richness of imagination influenced everything de la Mare wrote, emphasizing his frequent depiction of childhood as a time of intuition, deep emotion, and closeness to spiritual truth.

As a poet, de la Mare is often compared with Thomas Hardy and William Blake for their respective themes of mortality and visionary illumination. His greatest concern was the creation of a dreamlike tone implying a tangible but nonspecific transcendent reality. This tone has drawn many admirers, though it has also drawn criticism of the poet's indulgence in an undefined sense of mystery without systematic acceptance of any specific doctrine.

For his inventive extravagance, critics sometimes label de la Mare an escapist who retreats from accepted definitions of reality and the relationships of conventional existence. His approach, however, profoundly explores the world he considered most significant—that of the imagination. In the *London Mercury*, J. B. Priestley favorably concluded in 1924 that de la Mare is "one of that most lovable order of artists who never lose sight of their childhood, but re-live it continually in their work and contrive to find expression for their maturity in it, memories and impressions, its romantic vision of the world" (34).

Much of his poetry evokes a numinous sensation of being between the worlds of the natural and the supernatural, without defining any particular religious or even moral framework. It is perhaps this, most of all, which makes his attitude contemporary even now. Peter Penzoldt called de la Mare a writer of "inconclusive" ghost stories (205); he can also be seen as a writer of inconclusive verse.

Les Daniels remarked of de la Mare's atmospheric stories that they "are so subtly done that the presence of the uncanny must be intuited from insufficient evidence" (92), and the same is the case with much of his verse. For the connoisseur (to borrow the name of one of his books) of the macabre who values ambiguity and indefiniteness over explicit horrors, de la Mare's poetry is a must.

As Scott Connors has pointed out: "de la Mare compared ghost stories to poetry, in that both required the reader to will himself to believe before he can be affected" and that "just as there exists 'poetical truth', so too in the ghost story do we encounter 'imaginative truth,' where atmosphere is of chief importance. Part of this involves the investiture of everyday 'characters, setting, scene, circumstances' with 'the gradual conviction that this workaday actuality of ours . . . may have queer and, possibly, terrifying holes in it" (319).

The frequent motifs of de la Mare's poetry are the times of day and their domestic rituals; the seasons and their fruits; the symbolic death and rebirth inherent in sleeping and waking, autumn and spring. A dozen poems employ "Winter" in the title; half-a-dozen more, "Snow." He several times used "Alone" as a title. He is fond of fanciful language, constrained in verse by tight forms. The variety of these forms in his work is one of its delights, making each poem seem fresh and different.

We can only indicate some general lines of his work here, by examining a fraction of his output—some lines of poems from *Collected Poems* (1959; rpt. 1979) (which, despite the title, is a *selection* that contains no poems primarily intended for children). It is difficult to separate de la Mare's weird verse from his general verse; the distinction may be a purely artificial one, for all his poetic work is imbued with a remarkable delicacy of description and suffused with a sense transcendence and enchantment.

His most famous poem is "The Listeners," which headed his first mature adult collection in 1912:

> "Is there anybody there?" said the Traveller,
>   Knocking on the moonlit door . . .

Since this poem is widely available and easily accessible, I will not analyze it at length; but two things may be said of it. Firstly, the question posed by the traveler can be taken as a summation of the effect de la Mare continually aims for throughout his work. Secondly, the poet deftly takes the reader on a journey whereby the individual reader identifies with, and in a sense *becomes*, the spectres. In "The Sunken Garden," the poet tells of a "green and darkling spot" where:

> Perchance a distant dreamer dreams;
> Perchance upon its darkening air
> The unseen ghosts of children fare,
> Faintly swinging, sway and sweep,
> Like lovely sea-flowers in the deep . . .

Occasionally de la Mare allows himself a quasi-Christian or conventionally spiritual image, as in "The Willow," where he says that the tree "praises God in her beauty and grace . . ." In some poems, a more central Christian theme is expressed, but as in "A Ballad of Christmas," which is about Herod, Pilate and Judas, a darker message is conveyed. The poem opens:

> It was about the deep of night,
>   And still was earth and sky,
> When in the moonlight, dazzling bright,

Three ghosts came riding by.

By the middle of the poem, the narrative has taken a grim tone:

> For bloody was each hand, and dark
>> With death each orbless eye;—
> It was three Traitors mute and stark
>> Came riding silent by.

Yet other poems bespeak a more pagan, polytheistic attitude, as in "They Told Me," whose tenor is similar to the lines of Frank Belknap Long's famous "Sonnet" ("The gods are dead. The earth has covered them . . ."):

> They told me Pan was dead, but I
>> Oft marvelled who it was that sang
> Down the green valleys languidly
>> Where the grey elder-thickets hang.
>
> Sometimes I thought it was a bird
>> My soul had charged with sorcery;
> Sometimes it seemed my own heart heard
>> Inland the sorrow of the sea.
>
> But even where the primrose sets
>> The seal of her pale loveliness,
> I found amid the violets
>> Tears of an antique bitterness.

Similarly, the mention of "elfland" in "Sallie's Musical Box" adds a magical touch:

> Once it made music, tiny, frail, yet sweet—
> Bead-note of bird where earth and elfland meet,
> Now its thin tinkling stirs no more, since she
> Whose toy it was, has gone; and taken the key.

"Sorcery" is a poem about Pan much akin in spirit to "They Told Me."

In "The Spark," the poet tells of a meteor striking Earth—some poetic correlate to the strange otherworldly body in Lovecraft's "The Colour of Space"?

> I saw in utter silence sweep
> Out of that darkening starless vault
> A gliding spark, as blanched as snow,
> That burned into dust, and vanished in
> A hay-cropped meadow, brightly green.
>
> A meteor from the cold of space
> Lost in earth's wilderness of air?—
> Presage of lightnings soon to shine
> In splendour on this lonely place?—

Ghosts in the classical sense are the subject of several poems, such as "The Spectre," "The Ghost" (there is more than one poem of this title), "The Captive," "The Revenant," "The Phantom," and "The Shade."

De la Mare's sequence of poems from Shakespeare includes one on Macbeth and one on Banquo, who famously appears as a ghost at the feast after being slain. "Macbeth" is depicted Medusa-like:

> Around his head like vipers all distort,
> His lock shook, heavy-laden, at each stride.
> If fire may burn invisible to the eye;
> O, if despair strive everlastingly;
> Then haunted here the creature of despair,
> Fanning and fanning flame to lick upon
> A soul still childish in a blackened hell.

And "Banquo" in the following chilling images:

> "Begone, thou shuddering, pale anomaly! . . .
> Thou knowest not now the limit of man's heart;
> He is beyond thy knowledge. Gaze not then,
> Horror enthroned with insanest light!"

However, many poems use ghostly imagery merely in passing, as in "A Robin," with its "Ghost-grey the fall of night, / Ice-bound the lane," and "Martins: September," with its

> A tiny, elfin ecstatic host . . .
> > And 'neath them, on the highway's crust,
> Like some small mute belated ghost,
> > A sparrow pecking in the dust.

And "A Sunrise," with its description of the night-mists thinning away: "Like wraiths, of light distilled, they seem— / Phantoms of beauty from a forgotten dream."

Likewise, in "Homesick," the poet refers to "the lone ghost in thee"; "The Voice" references a withered leaf being wafted on in the street as "like a wayless spectre"; and in "Twilight," the poet declares: "And out of solitude your very ghost / Steals through the scarce-seen shadow of your hair."

However, in most of de la Mare's poems ghosts are not simply conventional terrifying spectres of lost lovers, dead children, relatives, and so on, but pale, faint spirits—mere *suggestions* of life-after-life, or of fleeting and phantom aspects of life. In "Autumn," the ghost is a symbol of life draining away:

> Nought gold where your hair was;
> Nought warm where your hand was;
> > But phantom, forlorn,
> > Beneath the thorn,
> Your ghost where your face was.

"Winter Dusk" tells the story of a mother reading by the fireside to her two children:

> Dark frost was in the air without,
> > The dusk was still with cold and gloom,
> When less than even a shadow came
> > And stood within the room.

A faint and indefinite ghost indeed, to be "less than even a shadow"!

A horror of reality instils "Drugged," with its final disillusioned lines, as a drugged dreamer returns to his "flesh house" from the drugged frenzy in which he saw "Horrors, in beauty appareled": "Lone soul—in horror to see, / Than dream more meagre and awful, / Reality."

In a similar poem, "The Assignation," though this time with its subject persona in a haze of visions induced by fever rather than drugs, the poet sees a white horse on a hillside:

> Spellbound, I watched it—hueless man and tail
> Like wraith of foam upon an un-named sea;
> Until, as if at mute and inward hail,
> It raised its gentle head and looked at me—
>
> Eyes blue as speedwell, tranquil, morning-fair:
> It was as if for aeons these and I
> Had planned this mystic assignation there,
> In this lone waste, beneath that wintry sky . . .

In this case, the vision seems more good omen than bad. This poem reminds us that many of de la Mare's weird verses, even though filled at times with furtiveness and shadows, contain images of great beauty and realistic observation of nature.

The image of Death's omnipresence stalks countless of the poems, but a few examples will suffice. In "Hospital":

> Ghosts may be ours; but gaze thou not too closely
> If haply in chill of the dark, thou rouse to see
> One silent of foot, hooded, and hollow of visage,
>   Pause, with secret eyes, to peer out at thee.

Old age and death are thematically predominant in such poems as "I Sit Alone," "Even in the Grave," "Alone," "The Stranger," "Forests," "Never More, Sailor," and "The Hawthorn Hath a Deadly Smell," whose last stanza reads:

> Eyes of all loveliness—
> Shadow of strange delight,
> Even as a flower fades

Must thou from sight;
But, oh, o'er the grave's mound,
Till come the Judgement Day,
Wreathed shall with incense be
Thy sharp-thorned may.

One could cite innumerable further examples of the theme of death in de la Mare's poems. "A Sign" is about "the end of things coming" (that is, the inevitable descent of all life to the grave), as are "Dust to Dust," "When the Rose Is Faded," "The Death Dream," and "A Rose in Candelight." Likewise "Goodbye," with its closing lines:

Love of its muted music breathes no sigh,
Thought in her ivory tower gropes in her spinning,
Toss on in vain the whispering trees of Eden,
Last of all last words spoken is, good-bye.

Great poignancy on the subject is conveyed in a mere eight lines in "The House":

"Mother, it's such a lonely house,"
    The child cried; and the wind sighed.
"A narrow but a lovely house,"
    The mother replied.

"Child, it is such a narrow house,"
    The ghost cried; and the wind sighed.
"A narrow and lonely house,"
    The withering grass replied.

The melancholy sense of Death's ever-present threat to our frail lives is almost an obsessive theme with de la Mare, exemplified again in "Shadow":

The loveliest thing earth hath, a shadow hath,
A dark and livelong hint of death,
Haunting it ever till its last faint breath . . .
Who, then, may tell
The beauty of heaven's shadowless asphodel?

There is another poem of the same title, and in it the recurrent theme of transience: "Lurks there in every rose's sweet / A murderous whisper, *Fade must I?*" Moreover, the climax of "Faint Music" is: "All sounds to silence come." Again, in "Futility" we have another iteration of death as the implacable enemy:

> Doth not the summer faint at last?
> Do not her restless rivers flow
> When that her transient day is past
> To hide them in ice and snow?

De la Mare's poems are replete with sunsets, faded flowers, old houses, eerie moonlight, the cries of owls, lost happiness, and "ghosts . . . remote and chill / Waiting the moon's phantasmal fire" ("The Tryst"). Even the imagery of childhood, which crops up in many of his poems, usually represents a longing for things past and irretrievable. Amidst the many beautiful poems of nature, there is an increasing quotient of verses of sadness, such as "Never-to-Be," "Winter Dusk," "The Last Guest," "Never Yet," "Never Again," "In a Churchyard," "The Bourne," and "This Is the End."

One of de la Mare's most bizarre and apocalyptic poems is the long "Gloria Mundi" which opens:

> Upon a bank, easeless with knobs of gold,
>   Beneath a canopy of noonday smoke,
> I saw a measureless Beast, morose and bold,
>   With eyes like one from filthy dreams awoke,
> Who stares upon the daylight in despair
> For very terror of the nothing there.
>
> This beast in one flat hand clutched vulture-wise
>   A glittering image of itself in jet,
> And with the other groped about its eyes
>   To drive away the dreams that pestered it;
> And never ceased its coils to toss and beat
> The mire encumbering its feeble feet.

On a very few occasions de la Mare touches on cosmic imagery, which puts one in mind of an Algernon Blackwood or a Clark Ashton Smith. For instance, in "Euphrasy" we encounter the magnificent lines:

> And Despair lifted up
> His gaunt cavernous face;
> He said, "I see Suns
> Like wild beacons, in space;
> I cannot endure
> The blaze, dazzle, flare!"
> But the child—he saw only
> Faint stars glinting there.

De la Mare is quite capable of utilising familiar fantastical imagery, as in this stanza from "The Universe":

> In his dark eyes lay a wild universe,—
> Wild forests, peaks, and crests;
> Angels and fairies, giants, wolves and he
> Were that world's only guests.

In "The Mermaids," the poet declaims:

> Blow, blow winding shells;
> And the watery fish,
> Deaf to the hidden bells,
> In the waters plash;
> No streaming gold, no eyes,
> Watching along the waves,
> But far-blown shells, faint bells,
> From the darkling caves.

However, de la Mare rarely used such straightforward fantastical tropes. Most of his poems are subtle and indefinite (another way in which they resemble the stories of Blackwood, or even of Robert Aickman), suggesting the strange rather than bringing it fully into the light. Weirdly exotic imagery occurs occasionally, as in "Arabia":

> Hear her strange lutes on the green Banks

Ring loud with the grief and delight
Of the dim-silked, dark-haired Musicians
In the brooding silence of night.

Similarly exotic imagery is found in "Dreams":

Ev'n one who has little travelled in
This world of ample land and sea;
Whose Arctic, orient, tropics have been—
Like Phoenix, siren, jinn and Sidhe—
But of his thoughts' anatomy—
Each day makes measureless journey twain:
From wake to dream; to wake again.

And in "Queen Djenira":

They slide their eyes, and nodding, say
    "Queen Djenira walks today
The courts of the lord Pthamasar
    Where the sweet birds of Psuthys are."

One of his most straightforward poems dealing with a horrific
subject is "Fear," whose first and final stanzas are:

I know where lurk
The eyes of Fear;
I, I alone
Where shadowy-clear,
Watching for me,
Lurks Fear.

In marble hands
To where on high
The jewelled horror
Of his eye
Dares me to struggle
Or cry.

Another effective short poem of understated horror is "The Omen":

134   SPECTRAL REALMS

Far overhead—
The glass set fair—
I heard a raven in the air;
'Twixt roof and stars it fanning went,
And croaked in sudden dreariment.

Over the pages of my book
I, listening, cast a sidelong look,
Curtained the window; shut the door;
I turned me to my book once more;
But in that quiet strove in vain
To win its pleasure back again.

Other such short horrific poems well worth reading include "Unforeseen" and "Foreboding."

De la Mare's fondness for old-fashioned language has met a mixed reception among critics. One has written: "Within the space of a short poem, De la Mare could both convey 'the inexplicable mystery of sound' and parade his weakness for hackneyed whimsy. . . . The main obstacle for a generation raised on Eliot and Pound is this attachment to 'goblin language', the 'haths' and 'howsoevers', the 'shoon' so conveniently lit by the moon. Never let pass a 'hearken' or a ''tis' or an 'ever and anon'; don't say 'before' when you can say 'ere', use 'nigh' instead of 'near'" (Campbell). Some commentators also criticize the poetry for having an archness of tone more suitable for children's verse.

With *The Burning-Glass and Other Poems* (1946), critics perceived a falling off from the author's past artistic virtuosity, which he only periodically regained thereafter. It is generally agreed, however, that de la Mare was a skillful manipulator of poetic structure, a skill particularly evident in the earlier collections.

According to Henry Charles Duffin in his *Walter de la Mare: A Study of His Poetry* (1949), the "poetry of Walter de la Mare is not essentially either a criticism of life or (as some think it) an escape from life. It will fulfill both these functions for those who require them, but the primary end of de la Mare's poetry is to heighten life" (196).

Certainly, for the devotee of weird verse, de la Mare's collections offer a storehouse of spectral, weird, and exotic poems worth savoring one by one. His vast body of poetic work is richly deserving of further study. Truly, it can be said of de la Mare that, like the King of Never-to-be in his poem of the same title:

> . . . all his realm is foam and rain,
> Whispering of what comes not again.

Works Cited or Consulted

Adrian, Jack. "Walter de la Mare." in *St James Guide to Horror, Ghost & Gothic Writers.* ed. David Pringle. Detroit: St James Press, 1998. 174–77.

Briggs, Julia. "Walter de la Mare." In *The Penguin Encyclopedia of Horror and the Supernatural,* ed. Jack Sullivan. New York: Viking, 1986. 117–20.

Campbell, James. "A Kind of Magic." *Guardian* (10 June 2006). http://tinyurl.com/hcowc9t

Clute, John. "Walter de la Mare." In *Supernatural Fiction Writers,* ed. E. F. Bleiler. New York: Scribners, 1985. 497–503.

Connors, Scott. "Walter [John] de la Mare." In *Supernatural Literature of the World,* ed. S. T. Joshi and Stefan Dziemianowicz. Westport, CT: Greenwood Press, 2005. 319–21.

Daniels, Les. *Living in Fear: A History of Horror in the Mass Media.* 1976. New York: Da Capo Press, 1983.

de la Mare, Walter. *Collected Poems.* 1959. London: Faber & Faber, 1979.

Duffin, Henry Charles. *Walter de la Mare: A Study of His Poetry.* 1949. Freeport, NY: Books for Libraries Press, 1969.

Joshi, S. T. *Unutterable Horror: A History of Supernatural Fiction.* 2012. New York: Hippocampus Press, 2014.

Penzoldt, Peter. *The Supernatural in Fiction.* 1952. New York: Humanities Press, 1965.

Priestley, J. B. "Mr de la Mare's Imagination." *London Mercury* 10 (May 1924): 34. Rpt. in *Figures in Modern Literature.* London: John Lane, 1928.

Reviews

A Dreamer's Rimes

J.-M. Rajala

H. P. LOVECRAFT. *Fungi from Yuggoth: An Annotated Edition.* Edited by David E. Schultz. Illustrated by Jason C. Eckhardt. New York: Hippocampus Press, 2017. 288 pp. $45.00 hc (limited edition).

It sometimes takes a long period of gestation until an editorial undertaking can be brought to a satisfactory conclusion. When, in 1937, August Derleth and Donald Wandrei began collecting H. P. Lovecraft's letters for publication, they could hardly have foreseen that it would take the better part of four decades for their projected selection of the correspondence to see print. And yet, in hindsight, that extended delay can be shown to have been to the benefit of their compilation, which thus was allowed to grow and be transmuted in the process of its protracted making; being hardened, as it were, in the alternating heat of the refining crucible, now cold and now hot, as the attention of the editors could be channeled to the work amid other labors.

Thus it may also be with this less bulky tome of Lovecraftiana. David E. Schultz's copiously annotated and carefully prepared edition of the cosmic Yankee's poetical magnum opus, *Fungi from Yuggoth,* has likewise long been promised, and after decades of expectancy and minor eleventh-hour delays in typesetting, it has now emerged fully fashioned and luminous from the forge, illustrated by Jason C. Eckhardt and issued by a publishing house that, well established though it may now be, was still only a distant sight in the horizon when the work was first conceived. Indeed, I believe the book was begun in earnest before this reviewer had scarcely heard of the author or of the poem. But now that its publication is finally at hand, I have had the pleasure of acquainting again myself with the verses and their background in a new setting while examining what this edition *de luxe* holds in store.

The book is divided into four or five parts, between which the relatively slender frame of the poem itself is extended by supplementary matter to span close to 300 pages of printed text. We thus have before ourselves a substantial volume that invites repeated perusal. Does the original work warrant such lavish attention? The question must be answered emphatically in the affirmative. As a poetic product of its maker and as a self-contained entity the cycle stands supreme and calls for a quarto of its own, set apart and elevated from the rest of Lovecraft's verse, a large proportion of which is frankly not especially meritorious, as he himself well knew. But here inspiration subjugated craft, the sonnet form perhaps providing the perfect vehicle whereon his metrical instinct could only serve by laying a solid foundation upon which creative impulse might blaze untrammeled. There have, of course, been other editions of the poem, but none nearly as ambitious as the present one nor at this point recent or easily obtainable, so that the book is doubly welcome: both in its transmission of the text—in more forms than one, as will be seen—and in its elucidation.

Lovecraft's own words have been wisely accorded primacy, and the book opens with the first of the thirty-six loosely related sonnets that *Fungi from Yuggoth* ultimately came to comprise. They have been laid out so that each sonnet encompasses one spread, its numbered heading and an accompanying illustration placed on the even page, followed by the octavo and the sestet on the opposing page. As far as the written word is concerned, the status of the three dozen "Fungi" is more or less straightforward. To simplify the matter—the more complex details are explained in the book's editorial essay—Lovecraft's authoritative typescript has fortunately survived, serving here as the copy text; variants found in the major published appearances of the sonnets are recorded in an appendix. Aside from textual accuracy, Lovecraft would no doubt have approved of the edition's Caslon typeface—a design thoroughly familiar to Lovecraft from books printed in his beloved eighteenth century—as well as the now rarely employed typographical detail of the st ligature that is featured throughout the book.

Fungi from Yuggoth is the kind of work that genuinely demands a pictorial counterpart, and the book is duly graced by Jason C. Eckhardt's artwork. For many of those who have delved more deeply into the life and works of the sage of Providence either during or in the immediate aftermath of what was perhaps the golden age of Lovecraft scholarship, Eckhardt's work has probably become permanently associated with them, so that the choice of the illustrator for a volume whose roots go back to that burgeoning phase is a most appropriate one. The style of the drawings is suitably dreamlike and restrained, augmenting the poem in a harmonious mood while running the gamut from quintessential New England steeples to realms beyond mortal ken as the focus of the poem shifts. The artist's sympathy to Lovecraft's vision can be gauged from such details as the befitting selection of a view from Providence's Prospect Terrace to epitomize one of the sonnets. Aside from Eckhardt's fine depictions of the sequence, a few more ornamental pieces can be found scattered through the rest of the book as title page and other devices, and Schultz's commentary following the poem is additionally interspersed with a handful of miscellaneous facsimiles relevant to the discussion.

Following the illustrated text the original holograph draft is reproduced, this being a perfect example of Lovecraft's self-avowed method of composition, full of crossed-out words, lines, even whole stanzas. His distinct script holds a fascination of its own, an almost—dare I say it?—magical or occult quality. For someone like myself the actual manuscript, with its bewildering array of emendations and, on one page, an outpouring of notes for sonnets that at that point had yet to be written, is of absorbing interest and makes for captivating viewing and reading. Some of the discarded lines reveal aspects of the finished poem that are not apparent in the final wording, and I can anticipate returning to decipher these pages for many a moment. The draft also records the composition dates of the poem, and it is a remarkable fact indeed if the first set of fourteen sonnets was written—and the general appearance of the manuscript does not suggest otherwise—on the single day of 27 December 1929. Those with less keen eyesight need not fear, as the more notable of the rejected readings (those that have not been wholly obliterated) are given in the notes on the individual sonnets.

The purely editorial portion of the volume—which claims the greater part of it—is divided into two parts of different intent but slightly overlapping in their content, augmented by a number of appendices, as well as the ubiquitous (but make no mistake, quite useful) bibliography, and an index of titles and first lines. The section next to the manuscript facsimile, titled "Dim Essences," consists of an essay where the road to the *Fungi* is mapped out, treating in six sub-sections such matters as the origins of and possible influences upon the poem, and facets of its form, content, and publication history. (That last mentioned is of some complexity in itself.) Lovecraft was often his own most cogent, if also the severest, critic and explicator, and the essay is backed up with several illuminating selections from his letters and other writings. As a layman I found Schultz's discussion of the prosody of the poem to be particularly helpful, and concur in the assessment that Lovecraft here consciously chose to avoid his earlier trappings of following too rigidly the theoretical confines of any given metrical form, instead letting poetic feeling reign over strict adherence to the traditions of the sonnet. Liberated from the shackles of following inflexibly a meter for prosody's sake, he finally achieved what he had in youth often vainly sought. Schultz is also clearly correct in pointing out that the work Lovecraft did on an (ultimately unpublished) poetry manual, which was then being prepared by his long-standing amateur journalist friend Maurice W. Moe, was a signal impetus for the composition of *Fungi from Yuggoth*—indeed, it is demonstrated that Lovecraft himself recognized that it was so.

Another question that Schultz considers is the oft-discussed one of whether or not the poem exhibits narrative continuity beyond the first three sonnets. To my mind, Schultz here dispels once and for all the notion that it was intended or should be read as a coherent chronicle, although that is not to say that there is no unity of a different kind to be found. (The fact that Lovecraft connected the sonnets by attaching to them the overall but at the same time enigmatic title suggests as much.) Lacking a conclusive statement uttered by the author of the poem, the final section of the essay probably elucidates its unity and narrative thrust—or lack thereof—as much as it is possible to do. It would, in any case, probably be a mistake to wish for the initial fragment of a plot, such as it may be, to extend through the whole cycle, rather than to enjoy the sonnets as a series of kaleidoscopic images of weirdness, poignancy, and what Lovecraft termed "strange shadow." Let us not forget that it was his explicit opinion in later years that plot is a negligible element in weird writing, subservient to the overarching mood to be conveyed.

And there is more. Roughly a quarter of the book is devoted to a substantial section modestly titled "Notes." It is here that a discussion of the somewhat perplexing and unexplained title of the cycle is postponed, and I was not left unenlightened. The analogy of Lovecraft's subsequent usage of the plural "fungi" with Baudelaire's *Fleurs du mal* is a keen observation, and one that had not occurred to me. In many ways the poem stands at the crossroads of Lovecraft's adult work, simultaneously embodying notions found in earlier stories and hinting at ideas that later found, or might have found, expression in subsequent tales. Beside sundry other observations, these editorial notes supply the tangible references for these interconnections. The concluding appendices, in addition to the features already described, contain an annotated transcription of the set of notes by Lovecraft mentioned above (found on a page of the manuscript draft), the abortive and now well-known fragment where the beginning of the poem has been written out as a story, a chronology of the published appearances of the sonnets, and facsimiles of both of Harold S. Farnese's musical settings of two of them. (As far as I am aware, only one of the latter has previously been reproduced.)

If there is an acolyte of Lovecraftiana who has somehow yet to read the poem—from the printed page and with proper care, at any rate—he can well start with this book. Schultz's editorial remarks will in such a case hint at the direction of what to read next; that is, the few other products of the unexpected flowering of Lovecraft's poetic impulse at the close of the third decade of the twentieth century, of which the sonnet cycle was the brightest bloom. It may be noted that in its way that outpouring, too, required a long period of apparent dormancy for the great work eventually to issue.

This brief appraisal is not the place to consider the individual and varying merits of the sonnets, but I can safely conclude by baldly stating that H. P. Lovecraft was much too modest in claiming that he had "no real poetic ability." Most of us may never quite attain, except in fleeting moments, his fantastic vision of a world imbued with special meanings and dreamlike wonder, a world where the weird might impinge upon even so seemingly an innocent act as pigeon-flying; but I at least am grateful that in *Fungi from Yuggoth* he painted for posterity glimpses of those vistas, and—to pick just one example—left us with such unforgettable pictures as that suggested by the lines "crushing what he chanced to mould in play, / The idiot Chaos blew Earth's dust away." In its imagery, passing from wistful mirages and gardens of half-familiar strangeness to cosmic horrors spanning worlds known and unknown, the poem remains a potent and lasting statement of which this edition will elicit fresh readings.

The Ghostly Verses of the Science Fiction Poetry Association

Michael J. Abolafia

SHANNON CONNOR WINWARD, ed. *Eye to the Telescope.* Issue No. 22 (October 2016): "Ghosts." Science Fiction Poetry Association. http://eyetothetelescope.com/archives/022issue.html

The contemporary speculative poetry world throngs and seethes with energy, and it would not be a great exaggeration to suggest that a renaissance in miniature is today well underway. Publications like *Spectral Realms, Skelos, Xnoybis, The Audient Void, Weird Fiction Review, Eternal Haunted Summer,* and seemingly countless others have vivified an already powerful genre whose genealogy was profoundly contoured by Clark Ashton Smith, H. P. Lovecraft, Donald Wandrei, Frank Belknap Long, and, even earlier, the Graveyard Poets of the late eighteenth century. S. T. Joshi's exemplary, groundbreaking studies of supernatural verse—best represented by his comprehensive retrospective anthology, with Steven J. Mariconda, *Dreams of Fear: Poetry of Terror and the Supernatural* (Hippocampus Press, 2013), as well as his hallmark genre study, *Emperors of Dreams: Some Notes on Weird Poetry* (P'rea Press, 2008)—have codified the importance of a constellation of often under-examined subfields of speculative poetry (including weird and fantastical poetries, which often complexly incorporate the ghostly).

Eye to the Telescope, the online periodical of speculative poetry published by the venerable Science Fiction Poetry Association, remains one of the most expertly curated magazines in the field. Its themed October 2016 issue (#22), "Ghosts," edited by Shannon Connor Winward, is a moving and wide-ranging collection of spectral verses that largely succeed in channeling the ghostly in singularly imaginative and even untrodden ways. These cartographies of hurt and wonder, encompassing a variety of themes, affects, times, spaces, settings, and poetic forms, embody the metaphysical portents, strange spells, and supernatural philtres that animate the ghostly encounter. When taken in totality, these twenty-seven poems of dispossession and disappearance— the *élan vital* of spectral poetry—serve as object lessons on the infinite possibilities of the haunted and the haunting.

Winward's concise introductory note establishes the issue's novelty and its innovative sensibilities: "Though the quality of submissions was overwhelmingly strong," she explains, "I favored those that challenge the old ghost story tropes we are used to. Through *Eye to the Telescope*, the Science Fiction Poetry Association aims not just to feature speculative poetry but to define and then redefine it—to bring the poetry of the future into sharper focus here and now. Thus, the poems in this 'Ghosts' issue posit unusual, unexpected visions of afterlife." These poems deftly subvert and upend the "old ghost story tropes" characteristic of much mediocre supernatural poetry. L. W. Salinas's inaugural "Tulpa," as the title implies, considers the ghostly from a distinctly mystical perspective: a "tulpa" is a being or entity generated by virtue of mental discipline and spiritual purity. The poem adroitly considers the hauntology of writing itself, summoning the fragility of memory to evoke the frailty of writing: "If ghosts are the memory of a person bound to a place, / then what are words bound to paper but another form of ghost?" Salinas's poem posits words as eerie doppelgängers of the self, as specters of the mind: "I am here, I am alive, yet you see my ghosts with each line. / Wild spirits birthed from my mind and hands that you invited in." We are, in the end, "surrounded by spirits captured in paper and letters"—an uncanny "death of the author" in which the words take on *sui generis* existences of their own. Holly Lyn Walrath's "Hart Island" locates *revenance* in New York City's surely haunted potter's field—the Bronx island is overflowing with spirits, and the ghostly speaker's monologue feels like a plaintive yearning for rest, since, like Charon crossing the river Styx, "The ferry brings more each day." This poem exemplifies the spectral potentialities in all places—including on the outskirts of a hyper-urban metropolis.

Suzan Pickford's "Be My Geist," a sonorously stunning villanelle, marshals serious heft in its psychologically expressive concluding lines: "haunted by remnants hidden deep in your closet / it's no wonder you lost it, perplexed by the vortex." "Fevered Ream," an imagistically impressive prose-poem by Daniel R. Jones, is spirited and almost cinematic, and one of the most original pieces in the issue. The first paragraph is worth quoting in full: "Against a heat-lightning veneer of 130-thread count you slip from your die-cast sarcophagus comatose to ghost, soul tethered to body like a dangling tooth a child is not willing to yank . . ." The scalpel of Jones's language gleams brightly; his rhythmic, breathless, and expectant clauses and the images that limn them are stirring: "You burn blue across an Elysian nebula hung high between the star of Bethlehem and another." The poem's valedictory image is too scintillating and surprising to overtly unfold in this review—I wouldn't want to spoil it: it is absolutely worth your time.

Joe Nazare's taut, crawly "Hex Machina" is an efficient, thematically interesting techno-spectral extravaganza. "The cutting edge" "scythes" through society, Nazare writes, to the end of "reconstruct[ing] damaged cells." What results is something that exceeds that bounds of what can and should be—a ghostly apocalypse in which "Autumn trees continuously rebloomed, loosing a barrage of foliage; / Putrefying foodstuff refreshed, spilling from trashcan cornucopia." The last stanza is an exercise in the narrative possibilities of speculative poetry: in a mechanically apropos fashion, the poem's persona explains, "In a topsy-turvy world of apocalyptic abundance, the machines / Were now in the ghost, the supernatural nanotechnologized." The poem's clever ghostification of the technological is an idea that lives up to the editor's commitment to "unusual, unexpected visions of the afterlife." Christina Sng's "Ghost Month" is a compelling and condensed free-verse poem that carries faint echoes of Ezra Pound's imagism, as expressed in works like "In a Station of the Metro." Andrea Blythe's "Summer Hauntings" is noteworthy for its freeform, processional character and its fascinating treatment of the material aspects of the ghostly: "Even the ghosts / collapse over clotheslines and tree branches, dripping / like clocks in a Dalí painting, all / their footsteps and whisperings, cupboard slamming and shadowing / stilled by the oppression of the hot night."

Jessica J. Horowitz's "Romance" and Lauren McBride's untitled poem are moving in their economy and their concentrated genuine feeling, while Ann K. Schwader, a modern master of weird poetry, contributes a science fictional verse of interstellar phantoms: "Planetfall unlatched our clamshells. / Thawing into dust & spirit, we persisted . . . / Against a sun that spawns no shadows, drifting as we must . . ." John W. Sexton writes spiritedly about the elusive ghost moth; Rebecca Buchanan's ecologically inflected poem convenes the quiet persona of a ghost-watcher who finds the landscapes around her uncannily inhabited by animals; and Jane Yolen's incantatory "Embracing the Bear" meditates on the ghostly persistence and manifestations of trauma to spectacular effect. James Edward O'Brien's prose-poem "Séance at Black Horse Pike" is a ghost story in miniature: "There are spots where the past bleeds into the here-and-now like a cheap paint job," it begins—an "inhabited," convincing voice sustained throughout the poem. The issue's final piece, Alex Harper's "But after," is an emotive *meditatio* on the spectral cyclicality of our waking and dreaming lives.

The poems included in "Ghosts" have an admirable potency and synergy when read together, and they emblematize Northrop Frye's paradoxical assertion that "There is nothing really more ghostly than an absence of ghosts." That these poems skirt the Scylla and Charybdis of over-reliance on genre tropes is their greatest strength. Nanotechnological afterlives give way to anguished psychological portraitures of the ghostliness of trauma: a testament to the poems' multifaceted, ambitious and properly "speculative" qualities. These ghosts walk the endless hallways of our hearts. They dream of dying stars and the afterlife of light. And in their mourning, they sing.

Notes on Contributors

Michael J. Abolafia lives in New York City, where he studies English at Columbia University. His writing has appeared in *Sunlit*, *Supernatural Tales*, the *New York Daily News* online book blog, *Page Views*, and other venues. With David E. Schultz, he co-edited Park Barnitz's *The Book of Jade: A Critical Edition* for Hippocampus Press. With Alex Houstoun, he assumes coeditorship of *Dead Reckonings* in 2017.

Ross Balcom lives in southern California. His poems have appeared in *Beyond Centauri*, *inkscrawl*, *Poetry Midwest*, *Scifaikuest*, *Star*Line*, and other publications. He is a frequent contributor to *Songs of Eretz Poetry Review*.

David Barker has been a fan of weird literature all his life. Recently, his writings have appeared in *Fungi*, *Cyäegha*, and *Shoggoth.net*. In collaboration with W. H. Pugmire, David has had two books published by Dark Renaissance Books: *The Revenant of Rebecca Pascal* (2014) and *In the Gulfs of Dream and Other Lovecraftian Tales* (2015).

Leigh Blackmore has written weird verse since age thirteen. He has lived in the Illawarra, New South Wales, Australia, for the last decade. He has edited *Terror Australis: Best Australian Horror* (1993) and *Midnight Echo 5* (2011) and written *Spores from Sharnoth & Other Madnesses* (2008). A nominee for SFPA's Rhysling Award (Best Long Poem), Leigh is also a four-time Ditmar Award nominee. He is currently assembling an edition of *The Selected Letters of Robert Bloch*.

Benjamin Blake was born in 1985 and grew up in the small town of Eltham, New Zealand. He is the author of the poetry and prose collections *A Prayer for Late October*, *Southpaw Nights*, and *Reciting Shakespeare with the Dead*. His debut novel, *The Devil's Children*, was published in October 2016.

Adam Bolivar, a native of Boston, now residing in Portland, Oregon, has had his weird fiction and poetry appear in the pages of *Nameless*, the

Lovecraft eZine, *Spectral Realms*, and Chaosium's *Steampunk Cthulhu* and *Atomic Age Cthulhu* anthologies. His first book, *The Fall of the House of Drake*, was published by Dunhams Manor Press in 2015.

Jason V Brock has been widely published in anthologies, online, comics, and magazines (*Weird Fiction Review*, S. T. Joshi's *Black Wings* series, *Fangoria*, and many others). An award-winning filmmaker and publisher, he is also editor-in-chief of a website/print digest called *[NameL3ss]*. Along with his wife, Sunni, he is a herp, tech consultant, and health nut.

Jeff Burnett was first published in *Spectral Realms* #4. His influences are Clark Ashton Smith and Robert E. Howard. When not working, he spends his time writing poetry, playing mandolin, adventuring with his wife, and hunting the Ozark Highlands of Missouri.

Pat Calhoun works from an old house in Santa Rosa, California, that he shares with his wife, three cats, and a large collection of fantasy books. He wrote a column, "Weird Words," about vintage fantasy comics, that ran for fifteen years in Comic Book Marketplace and currently writes for the International Netsuke Society Journal. He is also busy editing *Weird and Wondrous: An Anthology of Fantasy Poems*, and writing a few of them as well.

Frank Coffman is professor of English, journalism, and creative writing at Rock Valley College in Rockford, Illinois. His primary interests as a critic are in the rise and relevance of popular imaginative literature across the genres of adventures, detection and mystery, fantasy, horror and the supernatural, and science fiction. He has published several articles on these genres and is the editor of Robert E. Howard's *Selected Poems*.

Ashley Dioses is a writer of dark fiction and poetry from Southern California. Her debut collection of dark traditional poetry, *Diary of a Sorceress*, is forthcoming from Hippocampus Press. Her poetry has appeared in *Weird Fiction Review*, *Spectral Realms*, *Skelos*, *Weirdbook*, *Gothic Blue Book*, and elsewhere.

Poems by **Kendall Evans** have appeared in *Weird Tales*, *Analog*, *Asimov's*, and other magazines. His stories have appeared in *Amazing*, *Weirdbook*, *Fantastic*, and elsewhere. His novel *The Rings of Ganymede*, a ring cycle in the tradition of Wagner's operas and Tolkien's *Lord of the Rings*, is now available (Alban Lake Books, 2014).

Ian Futter began writing stories and poems in his childhood, but only lately has started to share them. One of his poems appears in Jason V Brock's anthology *The Darke Phantastique* (Cycatrix Press, 2014), and he continues to produce dark fiction for admirers of the surreal.

Liam Garriock is a Scots author, poet, and flaneur whose influences include Arthur Machen, Franz Kafka, J. G. Ballard, William Hope Hodgson, William S. Burroughs, Jorge Luis Borges, William Blake, and other iconoclasts and metaphysical surgeons. He lives in Edinburgh, presently conjuring up the ghosts of Brion Gysin and Burroughs.

Wade German's writings have appeared in journals such as *Fungi, Hypnos, Weirdbook, Weird Fiction Review,* and previous issues of *Spectral Realms.* His poetry has been nominated for the Pushcart, Rhysling, and Elgin awards and has received honorable mentions in Ellen Datlow's *Best Horror of the Year* anthologies. His collection *Dreams from a Black Nebula* was published by Hippocampus Press.

Norbert Gora is a twenty-six-year-old poet and writer from Poland. Many of his horror, science fiction, and romance short stories have been published in his home country. He is also the author of many poems in English-language poetry anthologies around the world.

Oliver B. Harris had an awakening to weird fiction while studying theoretical physics as an undergraduate in London, and was intrigued by the Lovecraftian potential of *extra dimensions* and *compactified spaces,* which has informed much of his own fiction. Two short stories of his have appeared in the London-themed "neo–Penny Dreadful" *One Eye Grey,* and he has self-published a novella, *The Dulwich Horror,* for Kindle. He lives in Devon (UK) and makes a living as an engineer.

Bram Stoker Award–nominated author **Chad Hensley** had his first book of poetry, *Embrace the Hideous Immaculate,* published in May 2014 by Raw Dog Screaming Press. His recent poetry appearances include the *Weirdbook* #32, *Cyäegha* #17, the Horror Writers Association Horror

Poetry Showcase III, *Audient Void* #2 and #3, and the first six issues of *Spectral Realms*. He has nonfiction in *Weird Fiction Review* #7 and *Fenris Wolf* #7.

Clay F. Johnson is an amateur pianist, devoted animal lover, and incorrigible reader of Gothic literature and Romantic-era poetry. Among other literary endeavors, he is currently working on a small collection of poems and short stories inspired by the haunting events that took place in the "year without a summer" of 1816 that gave birth to Mary Shelley's *Frankenstein*, Byron's "Fragment of a Novel" and "Darkness," and Polidori's *The Vampyre*.

Charles Lovecraft has written verse since 1975, greatly inspired by H. P. Lovecraft. As publisher-editor he began P'rea Press in 2007 to publish weird and fantastic poetry, criticism, and bibliography, and to keep traditional poetry forms alive (www.preapress.com). He has edited nineteen books. Charles has seen publication in *Nyctalops*, *Eldritch Tales*, *Pablo Lennis*, *Weird Fiction Review*, *Spectral Realms*, *The Poet's Press*, *Black Wings IV*, and *Beyond the Cosmic Threshold*.

John J. Mundy's poems first appeared in *Spectral Realms*. His first published short story, a grim little tale of alchemy and the Black Pilgrimage, appears in the Mark Samuels tribute anthology *Marked for Death*, edited by the indefatigable Justin Isis. His literary heroes are H. P. Lovecraft, Jorge Luis Borges, and the late great Friedrich Dürrenmatt. He has considerable admiration for the macabre poetry of Joseph Payne Brennan while finding an unending source of inspiration in Lovecraft's wonderful *Fungi from Yuggoth*.

D. L. Myers's poetry has appeared in previous issues of *Spectral Realms*. His influences include H. P. Lovecraft, Clark Ashton Smith, Robert E. Howard, George Sterling, Algernon Blackwood, and Arthur Machen. He dwells among the mist-shrouded hills and farms of the Skagit Valley in the Pacific Northwest with his partner and a pack of demon badger hounds.

K. A. Opperman is a poet with a predilection for the strange, the Gothic, and the grotesque, continuing the macabre and fantastical tradition of such luminaries as Poe, Clark Ashton Smith, and H. P.

Lovecraft. His first verse collection, *The Crimson Tome,* was published by Hippocampus Press in 2015.

First published in *Lovecraft Annual* No. 4, **Manuel Pérez-Campos** is currently preparing a collection of his poetry in addition to a collection of essays on H. P. Lovecraft. His professional background is in psychotherapy. Born in Santiago, Cuba, of Lebanese-Spanish descent, he now lives in Bayamón, Puerto Rico.

W. H. Pugmire likes to follow Poe's example and plant poetry into his weird fiction. His sonnet sequence, "Songs of Sesqua Valley," appeared in *Sesqua Valley and Other Haunts* (Delirium Books, 2003). He is now at work on "Sonnets of an Eldritch Bent."

J.-M. Rajala works professionally as a software engineer and devotes bits of his spare time to literary research on authors of weird fiction and poetry, in particular H. P. Lovecraft, Clark Ashton Smith, and Ambrose Bierce. Distillations of his work have appeared in the journals *Lovecraft Annual* and *Weird Fiction Review.* He lives in southern Finland.

Nathaniel Reed was born, raised, and currently lives in Northwest Indiana. Recently graduated, he teaches high school earth/space science, environmental science, and biology. Reed previously appeared in the fifth issue of *Spectral Realms.*

Jessica Amanda Salmonson is a recipient of the Lambda Award, ReaderCon Certificate, and World Fantasy Award. She has written novels such as *Anthony Shriek* and *The Swordswoman;* short story collections such as *A Silver Thread of Madness, The Eleventh Jaguarundi,* and *The Deep Museum;* and has a poetry collection forthcoming from Hippocampus Press, *The Ghost Garden and Further Spirits.*

Ann K. Schwader lives and writes in Colorado. Her most recent collections are *Dark Energies* (P'rea Press, 2015) and *Twisted in Dream* (Hippocampus Press, 2011). Her *Wild Hunt of the Stars* (Sam's Dot, 2010) and *Dark Energies* were Bram Stoker Award finalists. She is also a 2010 Rhysling Award winner, and was the Poet Laureate for NecronomiCon Providence 2015.

Darrell Schweitzer's two serious poetry collections are *Groping toward the Light* and *Ghosts of Past and Future*. He hopes to have a third, exclusively weird collection out soon. His next book will be *The Threshold of Forever*, a collection of essays and reviews. He used to edit *Weird Tales*.

John Shirley's books include the novels *Demons*, *The Other End*, and *Bleak History*; his short story collections include *Black Butterflies* (which won the Bram Stoker Award) and *Lovecraft Alive!*, a collection of Lovecraftian stories from Hippocampus Press.

Claire Smith is a regular contributer to *Spectral Realms* (issues 1, 2, and 4). She has also recently been published in *The Night Café* (Alban Lake Publishing, 2016) and been featured in the journals *Trysts of Fate* and *Illumen*. She holds an MA in English from the Open University and currently lives in Cheltenham, Gloucestershire, UK.

Farah Rose Smith is a poet, fiction writer, and artist from Providence, R.I. She is the founder and editor of *Mantid Magazine* and the creative director of Grimoire Pictures. Her work, which often focuses on the surreal and avant-garde, has been recognized at film festivals, receiving accolades in both experimental film and screenwriting.

Oliver Smith is a visual artist and writer from Cheltenham, UK. His poetry has appeared in *Spectral Realms*, *Eye to the Telescope*, and *Illumen*. His fiction has been published in anthologies by, among others, Ex Occidente Press and The Inkermen. Much of his previously published short fiction and poetry is now collected in *Basilisk Soup and Other Fantasies*.

Christina Sng is a poet, writer, and artist. Her work has received nominations in the Dwarf Stars and Rhysling Awards as well as honorable mentions in *The Year's Best Fantasy and Horror*. She is the author of several chapbooks, and her first two full-length collections, *Astropoetry* (Alban Lake Publishing) and *A Collection of Nightmares* (Raw Dog Screaming Press), are slated for 2017.

Ronald Terry earned a B.A. and M.A. in English from the University of Southern Mississippi, where he wrote his M.A. thesis on the poetry of

Ted Hughes. He published his first poem in 1980; since then his poems have appeared in many print and online publications such as *Poetrybay*, *Dead Snakes*, *Night Cry*, *Space and Time*, *The Horror Zine*, *Star*Line*, among others.

Richard L. Tierney's *Collected Poems* appeared from Arkham House in 1981. A later volume of poetry was published as *Savage Menace and Other Poems of Horror* (P'rea Press, 2010). Tierney is also the author of *The Winds of Zarr* (Silver Scarab Press, 1975), *The House of the Toad* (Fedogan & Bremer, 1993), and many other works of horror and fantasy fiction.

Kyla Lee Ward's latest release is *The Land of Bad Dreams* (P'rea Press, 2011), a collection of dark poetry. Her novel *Prismatic* (Lothian, 2006) won an Aurealis and her work on RPGs includes *Demon the Fallen* (White Wolf Games Studio, 2002). Short fiction, films, and plays—she's been there, as well as a whole lot of cemeteries.

M. F. Webb recently returned to writing from a two-decade long, journalism-induced hiatus. Her poetry has appeared in previous issues of *Spectral Realms,* and her fiction in *Latchkey Tales.* A Texas transplant, she has made her home in Seattle for the past seventeen years. Her great-great-great-grandmother was a Poe.

Michelle Claire White is a passionate poet who draws her inspiration from ancient mythology, folktale, and esoteric symbolism. With a background drawn from studies of religion and literature at the University of Sydney, her poetry is inspired by the Romantics and imbued with their love of nature and fascination for pre-Christian mythologies. This is her first appearance as a published poet.

Mary Krawczak Wilson has written poetry, fiction, plays, articles, and essays. She was born in St. Paul, Minnesota, and moved to Seattle in 1991. Her most recent essay appeared in the *American Rationalist.*

www.ingramcontent.com/pod-product-compliance
Lightning Source LLC
Chambersburg PA
CBHW060759050426
42449CB00008B/1451